VEGGIES
& FISH

VEGGIES & FISH

Inspired New Recipes for Plant-Forward Pescatarian Cooking

BART VAN OLPHEN

Photographs by David Loftus

THE EXPERIMENT

NEW YORK

VEGGIES & FISH: *Inspired New Recipes for Plant-Forward Pescatarian Cooking*
Copyright © 2020 by Bart van Olphen
Photographs copyright © 2020 by David Loftus and Mitchell van Voorbergen
Translation copyright © 2021 by The Experiment, LLC

Originally published in the Netherlands as *Veggies & Fish: Ruim 80 Visrecepten met groente in de hoofdrol* by Fontaine Uitgevers in 2020. First published in English in North America in revised form by The Experiment, LLC, in 2021.

The Experiment, LLC | 220 East 23rd Street, Suite 600 | New York, NY 10010-4658
theexperimentpublishing.com

This book contains the opinions and ideas of its author. It is intended to provide helpful and informative material on the subjects addressed in the book. It is sold with the understanding that the author and publisher are not engaged in rendering medical, health, or any other kind of personal professional services in the book. The author and publisher specifically disclaim all responsibility for any liability, loss, or risk—personal or otherwise—that is incurred as a consequence, directly or indirectly, of the use and application of any of the contents of this book.

The Experiment's books are available at special discounts when purchased in bulk for premiums and sales promotions as well as for fund-raising or educational use. For details, contact us at info@theexperimentpublishing.com.

Library of Congress Cataloging-in-Publication Data

Names: Van Olphen, Bart, author. | Loftus, David, photographer.
Title: Veggies & fish : inspired new recipes for plant-forward pescatarian
  cooking / Bart van Olphen ; photographs by David Loftus ; styling by
  Inge Tichelaar.
Description: New York : The Experiment, [2021] | Originally published in the Netherlands as Veggies & Fish by Fontaine Uitgevers in 2020. Includes index.
Identifiers: LCCN 2021022129 (print) | LCCN 2021022130 (ebook) | ISBN
  9781615198344 | ISBN 9781615198351 (ebook)
Subjects: LCSH: Cooking (Fish) | Pescatarian cooking. | Vegetarian cooking.
  | Cooking (Fish) | LCGFT: Cookbooks.
Classification: LCC TX747 .V327 2021 (print) | LCC TX747 (ebook) | DDC
  641.6/92–dc23
LC record available at https://lccn.loc.gov/2021022129
LC ebook record available at https://lccn.loc.gov/2021022130

ISBN 978-1-61519-834-4
Ebook ISBN 978-1-61519-835-1

Cover design by Beth Bugler
Text design by Tijs Koelemeijer
Food styling by Inge Tichelaar
Translation by Laura Vroomen

Manufactured in China

First printing October 2021
10 9 8 7 6 5 4 3 2 1

CONTENTS

RECIPES

INTRODUCTION
VEGETABLES & FISH

Years ago, when I was at culinary school and working in restaurant kitchens, it was simple: When you put together a dish, you'd start by choosing your meat, game, poultry, or fish, preferably in a generous portion of 6½ ounces (180 grams) or more. Next, you turned your attention to the sauce, and only then did you start thinking about vegetables and a starchy element. Both were a kind of filler, if anything, and sometimes they didn't even complement each other very well. And the seasonality and provenance of your ingredients were certainly not part of the equation. Fortunately, it's all totally different now.

Since entering the world of fish some fifteen years ago, I've seen many changes. Not only have people begun to appreciate vegetables a lot more, but we're also paying more attention to where products are sourced. At the same time, there's a growing group of consumers who, as a matter of principle, oppose factory farming. Similarly, awareness of fishing methods and fish farming is on the rise, and here, too, provenance plays a key role. And I've seen a difference in the way seafood is prepared and consumed.

In recent years, my culinary trips to Peru, Sri Lanka, Indonesia, Italy, and many other countries have inspired me to change the way I cook. I never really stopped to think about it, but vegetables gradually took on a more prominent role—in part because I wanted a healthier diet for me and my children, but also because I began to derive more pleasure from them. I was fascinated by the many different flavors, textures, and colors that vegetables provide. Without neglecting the fish, I took to experimenting with the abundance of the vegetable world. Where once I'd treated vegetables as a mere garnish—and later accorded them equal status with the proteins at the center of the plate—I now often turn to vegetables as the cornerstone of my recipes. Fish still plays an important role, but it's served in smaller portions.

The interesting thing about all this is that not only do the textures, flavors, and colors of vegetables combine fabulously well with fish, but the preparation and cooking times of the two aren't too dissimilar. In fact, the worlds of veggies and fish have a lot in common. Maybe more than you'd think. Obviously, both offer endless variety. Many fish and vegetables can be eaten raw, while cooking them is quick and easy. They're packed with healthy nutrients and are best eaten when in season. And to cap it all, they're absolutely delicious. In short, you can create the tastiest vegetable and fish dishes in no time at all.

The book is organized mostly by preparation techniques. The recipes, as always beautifully photographed by my dear friend and top photographer David Loftus, are a fun mix of cuisines from around the world and range from simple breakfast dishes (yup, you can have fish for breakfast!) to rich and festive dining. I hope this book will inspire you to eat more fish, like I do, but focus on the vegetables.

Bart van Olphen, June 2021

VEGETABLES, SEAWEEDS & HERBS

It's fascinating to see just how many vegetables there are. Big and small, in all colors of the rainbow, and with lots of different textures. And given the huge variety of flavors, there's so much you can do with them. Honestly, I can't think of a single vegetable that doesn't combine well with fish. But because this book is intended as a source of inspiration and not as a reference book, I'll limit myself to those vegetables that I like to combine with fish—preferably organic and seasonal, of course. I also welcome this opportunity to share my love of fresh herbs, as well as seaweeds and sea vegetables, which are widely seen as the food of the future.

VEGETABLES & FRUITS

Below is a list of the vegetables that I use the most in combination with fish. But this is just a start—there are so many others that lend themselves to tasty veggie-and-fish dishes.

ARTICHOKE
Striking because of its beautiful shape and especially its unique flavor, artichoke is one of my favorite vegetables. Artichokes can be cooked whole or turned with the hard outer leaves and the hairy inner choke cut away. The heart is soft, with a subtle flavor, but the leaves are good too, dipped in anchovy sauce (page 123), for example, and then scraped with your teeth. Canned or jarred artichoke hearts are an acceptable alternative to the fresh version of this thistle bud.

ASPARAGUS
White asparagus grows underground, green asparagus above ground. The white variety has to be peeled before preparation, the green one only trimmed. White asparagus has a soft and delicate flavor, while the green spears are stronger tasting and have a firmer texture. That's where the differences end. Boiled, grilled, or oven-roasted, both pair really well with fish (or else they wouldn't be in this book!).

You can tell whether asparagus is fresh by looking at the end of the stalk: It should be tender and not dry. And when you pick up a bunch and rub the stalks together, they should "squeak" a little (no, really!).

AVOCADO
Thanks to its rich and creamy flavor, this fruit is great raw, either coarsely chopped or mashed. When you buy an avocado, make sure it's ready to eat; you can also speed up the ripening process by placing an avocado in a brown paper bag with a banana. A dash of lemon or lime juice helps to retain the avocado's beautiful green color.

BEET
The earthy and sweet flavor of beets is a perfect complement for pickled or smoked fish with a tangy dressing. It's also fun to combine different colors, like red, yellow, and red-and-white striped Chioggia beets. Thinly sliced, they can be eaten raw, but they're also good boiled or oven-roasted.

BELL PEPPER

Different color bell peppers all have subtly different flavors. The green variety—which is harvested earlier—is slightly bitter; the yellow variety is less bitter and has a hint of sweetness; and the orange and red bell peppers are sweeter still. Bell peppers also add a pleasant crunch to dishes. They are delicious eaten raw, roasted, braised, or as the base of a robust sauce.

CARROT

All carrots pair well with fish. They're good eaten raw as well as boiled or steamed, but caramelized roasted carrots are my personal favorite. Roasting intensifies this root vegetable's natural sweetness and concentrates its flavor. Although usually orange in hue, green, purple, white, and yellow carrots are readily available, too.

CAULIFLOWER

Cauliflower has a distinct cabbage flavor—mild, with a hint of bitterness. Though white cauliflower is the most popular, the colored varieties (purple, green, and orange) are becoming more widely available, and provide a touch of vibrancy to your dish. Cauliflower is delicious paired with crab or lobster or served raw with a good anchovy sauce (page 123).

CHILE

Yellow, green, red—they all make an appearance in this book, from the extremely pungent ají amarillo from Peru to the milder jalapeño from Mexico. Chiles are central to curries, but they can also be used in countless other recipes. The amount of capsaicin determines how hot the chile is. To get the flavor but not the overpowering heat, remove the seeds before adding the chile to your dish.

CUCUMBER

Cucumber doesn't have a very distinctive flavor, which may be why it's such a satisfyingly fresh addition to many fish recipes. The seeds can be removed for a firmer texture. For a more concentrated flavor, diced cucumber can be sprinkled with salt and left to drain in a kitchen towel or sieve over a bowl in the fridge overnight.

EGGPLANT

You'll notice that I have a lot of love for eggplant. Its almost-meaty texture easily absorbs other flavors. It can be used in all kinds of ways, but it's best eaten cooked. Much of the flavor is in the skin, so I never remove it. But if you're not yet a fan, you can try it without the skin.

FENNEL

Fennel is my favorite vegetable match for fish. It contains the compound estragole, which gives it that delicious aniseed flavor. So does tarragon, another perfect combination (see page 14). Fennel can be used in all kinds of ways—raw, slowly braised, and everything in between. And don't forget to use the delicious green fronds!

GARLIC

This flavorful plant belongs to the same family as onions, leeks, and chives. I always try to get hold of green garlic. This bulb with its distinctive green stalk is more widely available these days and has a milder, subtler flavor than its more mature dried sibling. But don't let that stop you from using standard garlic that has been let dry. When sautéing onion and garlic as the basis of a dish, add the garlic last, as overcooking can make it bitter.

LEMON & LIME

Under a single heading, but only for convenience's sake, as they taste quite different. To my mind, limes have a fresher, fruitier aroma and a tangier flavor, while lemons taste a bit sharper. The juice of both citrus fruits can give your dish that extra kick it needs. The most concentrated flavor is actually in the rind, which is delicious grated onto a dish. Always opt for organic lemon and lime when you're using the zest or preserving.

LETTUCE

Lettuce is the collective name for leafy greens that are eaten raw. I like to switch things up and use different varieties including romaine, iceberg, curly endive, red leaf, green leaf, and butter. Some, like romaine and iceberg, can be grilled or pan-fried, too.

ONION

Yellow onions have a sharp flavor when raw, but long, slow cooking makes them deliciously sweet (see Pesce in Saor, page 167). Red onion is less sharp, which is why it's frequently added raw to salads. Shallots are mild and sweet with a hint of sharpness. All small fresh onions (like scallions and spring onions) can be eaten whole, greens and all, and work well raw in salads or scattered over soups.

POTATO

There are as many varieties as there are flavors. I'll keep it simple in this book and stick to starchy potatoes (such as russets or baking potatoes) and waxy potatoes (such as red-skin potatoes or fingerlings). The sweet potato, which I also love, is technically from a different family, but no less delicious. If you like to cook potatoes with their skins on, make sure to scrub them first with a brush and cold water. Potatoes can't be eaten raw, but prepared in any way, they are perfect with fish.

SPINACH

In this book I use baby spinach, mature spinach, and water spinach. Whichever you buy, make sure the leaves look fresh, are firm and crisp, and are thoroughly rinsed. The stalks should snap when you bend them. I use all varieties in hot dishes, and baby spinach in cold preparations.

TOMATO

Tomatoes are available in all shapes and sizes, flavors, and colors. The standard tomato is a bit bland (especially out of season) but—like canned tomato—excellent for soups and sauces. Beefsteak tomatoes, which are less watery and have fewer seeds, are good in salads and other cold preparations. The oval-shaped Roma or plum tomato has a fuller and sweeter aroma and is relatively dry. Unlike the varieties mentioned above, vine tomatoes are ripened on the vine and have a much fuller flavor. Finally, there's the cherry tomato. With great differences in the intensity of flavor, I often opt for the vine-grown variety.

ZUCCHINI

This firm vegetable comes from the same family as pumpkin and cucumber and has a subtle, neutral flavor and a soft texture after preparation. The beautiful flowers of the zucchini plant are delicious, too, and can be stuffed and then steamed or deep-fried (mozzarella-and-anchovy–stuffed flowers are a classic). Although zucchini are mostly green, yellow varieties are available, too.

SEAWEEDS & SEA VEGETABLES

The sea is full of fish and shellfish, but we often forget that it's home to countless plants, too. Plants that grow in salt water are known as seaweeds. They are essential for marine life, as they absorb carbon dioxide and produce oxygen. Their role is comparable to that of the rain forest on land. Seaweeds are available preserved in salt, dried, and occasionally fresh. Sea vegetables grow on land, near the ocean. They thrive in saline soil, which helps them survive along the coast and in brackish areas.

SEAWEEDS

DULSE
This red weed grows around the North Atlantic coast. When briefly fried in butter, dried dulse is reminiscent of bacon.

KELP
Kelp is a brown alga that grows in shallow waters. Atlantic Sea Farms, based in Maine, grows stunning native kelp. They diversify how coastal waters are used by providing a domestic, fresh, healthy alternative to imported seaweed, which currently makes up 90 percent of the seaweed used in the US. And they employ heritage lobster fishermen, teaching them a new way to work on the water while helping to restore the ocean's abundance.

NORI
Nori is best known as the seaweed wrapped around sushi rolls. It's crispy, savory, and light in texture.

SEA SPAGHETTI
The long strands of this brown seaweed grow along European coastlines and in the northeast Atlantic Ocean. It's creamy and briny, but acquires a nutty, savory flavor when baked.

WAKAME
Wakame has an intense and savory flavor. It can be used in the same way as leafy greens. This seaweed grows abundantly in the coastal areas of Japan, Korea, and China, as well as other temperate regions around the world. It is commonly used to make chuka wakame, a Japanese seaweed salad.

SEA VEGETABLES

ICE PLANT
The leaves of these green sea plants are covered in distinctive crystals. The flavor is sharp, briny, and bright, the texture crisp.

MARSH SAMPHIRE
This sea vegetable, also known as glasswort, is available year-round. The salty spears are good in fish and vegetable dishes, either raw or briefly sautéed.

SEA FENNEL
This briny version of the anise-like fennel is a true taste sensation. Also known as rock samphire, it's great in a mixed salad or as a garnish on hot dishes.

SEA LAVENDER
This leafy sea vegetable has a savory, briny flavor. The leaves can be used in the same way as other leafy vegetables, either raw or briefly sautéed.

HERBS

Fresh herbs can form the basis of a dish or provide the finishing touch. In this book, I use a wide variety of herbs—some with a very pronounced flavor, others that impart a more subtle note to the food.

CHERVIL
Chervil has a mild aniseed flavor. The sprigs, with their delicate leaf structure, can be used in salads and in hot fish dishes.

CHIVES
Chives have a mild onion flavor. The thin stalks are ideal for adding to dressings and salads or as a garnish. Chives should not be heated.

CILANTRO
You either love it or you hate it. Cilantro looks a bit like flat-leaf parsley, while its flavor could be described as a cross between parsley and lemon. I use it a great deal, especially in Asian-inspired dishes. It's hard to think of a Thai shrimp curry, for example, without cilantro.

DILL
Dill has soft and feathery leaves with a lovely aroma. The delicate flavor pairs exceptionally well with fish (think of gravlax, for instance). Use it sparingly, as too much dill can tip the balance of your dish.

MINT
This fresh herb has firm, oval-shaped leaves. The stalks are best discarded, while the leaves are either coarsely or finely chopped before use.

OREGANO
Oregano's tiny leaves are pungent, highly aromatic, and slightly sweet. I like to use oregano in baked and roasted dishes, and sometimes cold or raw.

Marjoram is a good substitute.

PARSLEY
This herb can be used in both hot and cold dishes. I personally prefer flat-leaf parsley to its curly counterpart, as it's more subtle. Parsley has a delicate aroma, so you can't really go wrong with it.

ROSEMARY
Given its strong aroma, this herb is not often paired with fish. But it works well with oilier fish like salmon. Rosemary is also good in lots of vegetable dishes and with potatoes, especially when oven-roasted.

SAGE
Sage has elongated velvety green leaves, and its full flavor pairs well with fish and sweeter vegetables such as carrot and sweet potato.

TARRAGON
Tarragon has elongated leaves with an aniseed aroma. This herb is wonderful in sauces, soups, and dressings. A great friend to fish!

THYME
Thyme has tiny aromatic leaves that impart a savory note to your dish. Use it sparingly, like rosemary, oregano, and sage, as the strong flavor can easily dominate.

FISH & SHELLFISH

Fish species can be classified in various ways, but I've chosen to organize them by family. Learning about the different species and families isn't just fun and informative; it's also particularly useful to know so that if necessary, you can substitute one fish for another in a given recipe. It's often surprisingly easy to do so within the same fish family. Fish is a supplier's market: The sea provides, and it's up to us to listen. If a particular variety you're after isn't available, you can substitute another one. It won't affect the taste or experience of that recipe. Below, I cover only sustainably caught species. When you buy fish, you should always look out for the MSC (Marine Stewardship Council) or ASC (Aquaculture Stewardship Council) label, or consult a seafood guide like the Monterey Bay Aquarium's Seafood Watch (seafoodwatch.org) or the Marine Stewardship Council (msc.org).

ROUND WHITE FISH

Cod and other white fish are hugely popular all over the world. They are available year-round, and despite variations in taste and texture, these fish are easily interchangeable in the recipes in this book.

COD

Cod has many different names. Dried and salted cod is known as saltfish, or bacalhau or baccalà in southern European cuisine. The dried, unsalted version, which is called stockfish, is widely used in Scandinavian countries.

HADDOCK

Haddock is a member of the cod family. It has black smudges behind its gills on either side of its body. Icelandic legend has it that the devil tried to grab the fish, but it managed to escape. This explains the "devil's thumbprint" on the side of its body.

HAKE

This fish has been hugely popular in the Mediterranean for some time now, and in recent years fresh and frozen hake has also caught on in the UK, where it's used for fish-and-chips. It has a nice firm texture and an off-white color.

POLLOCK

Much of the pollock consumed in the US is eaten in the form of fish sticks or fillets from the frozen foods section of the store. The fish is common in the cold waters around Alaska. The pollock's firm flesh is white and a little dry, but very flavorful.

WHITING

Whiting was long considered a "forgotten" fish, but it's starting to make a comeback. Its flesh is white, flaky, and soft, with a subtle flavor.

BASS

Bass, including sea bass, represent 40 percent of all fish species. With the exception of the Atlantic wolffish, the fish below—as well as other members of the bass family—are interchangeable in the recipes in this book. A fish's cooking time is determined by its size, not its species.

STRIPED BASS

Native to the Atlantic coast of North America, this fish has a silvery body with long, dark stripes running the length of its body. Available year-round, farmed striped bass has white flesh and a mild flavor, making it one of the most versatile fish to cook with.

ATLANTIC WOLFFISH

Despite its very different appearance, the wolffish (also known as the Atlantic catfish) is officially a member of the bass family. The fish has a delicate flavor and firm white flesh.

WALLEYE

This freshwater fish is another official member of the bass family and very common in the US, especially in the upper Midwest. Unlike many other freshwater fish, the walleye is widely used in gastronomy, mainly for its full yet neutral flavor and good texture. Another major selling point is the fact that it has relatively few bones, especially compared to many other freshwater fish.

OILY FISH

A fish is considered oily when its fat content is over 5 percent. The fatty acids not only make the fish extremely healthy eating but also give them their unique flavor. Oily fish can be small or large. And you'll find a surprising number of oily fish in tins, as the canning process preserves their flavor particularly well.

HERRING-LIKE FISH

ANCHOVY

Anchovies are found in both marine and brackish waters. Fresh anchovies are delicious pan-fried, while tinned and jarred anchovies are great for adding flavor to dishes or for topping salads.

HERRING

Herring is excellent smoked, pickled, or salted. Hollandse nieuwe, or soused herring, is celebrated in the Netherlands for its creamy texture and full flavor.

SARDINE

This fish owes its name to the Italian island of Sardinia. Sardines swim in large schools and have a strong flavor. When in season, they're widely available fresh. But the frozen and tinned varieties—if of good quality—are also great for cooking.

SPRAT

These little fish live in shallow coastal waters. They're delicious pan-fried but are also terrific smoked.

OTHER OILY FISH

MACKEREL

Mackerel live in large, tightly packed schools just below the water's surface. Their skin is a beautiful color, and their flesh is good pan-fried, smoked, or raw.

SWORDFISH

Currently, there are a few sustainable swordfish fisheries that allow us to obtain this firm, delicious fish. Its flesh is grayish white with a neutral flavor. Ideal for the novice fish consumer, it works really well pan-fried, grilled, and broiled.

TUNA

Tuna is often used as an all-inclusive term. But there are lots of different tuna varieties, each with its own distinct character and flavor. Below, I discuss those that are most widely available and sustainable. And although there's now one certified sustainable fishery for bluefin tuna, I'm not including that endangered species here because I believe we should leave them in peace for the foreseeable future.

ALBACORE TUNA

Also known as white tuna because of the color of its flesh (but not to be confused with escolar, also called white tuna), albacore has a firm bite and a full, fatty flavor. This species, which is still largely caught with pole and line by commercial fishermen, is available frozen and canned, and also fresh.

SKIPJACK TUNA

Fresh skipjack fillet is in no way inferior in quality to yellowfin or albacore, yet most of this delicious striped tuna tends to find its way into cans.

YELLOWFIN TUNA

Celebrated for its color and its distinctive yet mild flavor, it's now a mainstay in the kitchen thanks to culinary influences from countries like Japan, Peru, and the Mediterranean.

SALMON

Salmon is an anadromous fish, which means that after a few years at sea, the fish returns to the river where it was born to spawn in brackish or fresh water. Very popular in the United States, it is available year-round, fresh, smoked, frozen, and canned.

ARCTIC CHAR

You might not realize it, but arctic char is a member of the salmon family. This fatty fish with pink to red flesh, which is closely related to salmon and trout, is native to arctic and subarctic coastal waters. It is also farmed in Estonia, Finland, Iceland, Ireland, Norway, Sweden, and West Virginia.

ATLANTIC SALMON

No longer commercially caught in the wild, Atlantic salmon is now farmed on a large scale in Norway, Scotland, Chile, and Tasmania, to name a few, where it is raised in big cages at sea.

PACIFIC SALMON

Pacific salmon is exclusively caught in the wild, especially in the waters around Alaska and off the coast of British Columbia. The fishing season is May to September and the varieties available are chinook, chum, coho, pink, and sockeye.

TROUT

Trout is also a member of the salmon family. Wild trout isn't that easy to come by, as the overwhelming majority is farm raised these days. Trout is good baked, while the smoked variety can also be used in a range of recipes.

FLATFISH

As the name suggests, flatfish are flat. With the exception of the halibut, they spend most of their lives lying on their side. For the first few weeks after birth they look like regular fish, but then one of their eyes migrates to the other side of their head, and as a result, this side becomes the top.

FLOUNDER

Flounder refers to hundreds of different kinds of flatfish, including halibut, plaice, and sole. Most North American flounders are found along the Atlantic and Gulf coasts. The most common are summer flounder (fluke), winter flounder (American lemon sole), and southern flounder.

HALIBUT

The largest of all flatfish can grow up to 16 feet (5 m) in length. Pacific halibut is caught in Alaskan waters. The Greenland halibut, also known as black halibut or Greenland turbot, is the smaller version of the white or Atlantic halibut.

SOLE

Like many other flatfish, soles spend the day hiding below the sand on the bottom of the sea. At night, the fish swim with the current in search of food. Sole has a delicate and subtle flavor and a firm and succulent texture.

TURBOT

The name turbot derives from the old French tourbout, meaning "spinning top." And it's fair to say that the turbot looks a bit like one. It's an extremely delicate fish with beautiful bright white flesh and a full flavor. Turbot is now also responsibly and sustainably farm raised.

OTHER FISH

BLACK COD

Also known as sablefish, this fish is not actually a member of the cod family. It is commonly found in the North Pacific Ocean and is a delicacy in Japanese cuisine, where it is often marinated with sake and miso. Smoked sablefish is also a staple of American Jewish cuisine.

MAHI-MAHI

Widely consumed in the US, this fish is gaining in popularity in European countries, Australia, and Japan. It has a mild flavor, stronger than white fish like cod and haddock, but milder than swordfish.

MONKFISH

The monkfish is unique, with a wide mouth, a huge head, and a flat body that tapers off into a tail. The parts we consume are primarily the cheeks and tail. The texture of the flesh is exceptionally firm; its flavor, sweet and mild.

SHELLFISH

There are numerous species of shellfish, but I'll limit myself to those that are widely available. Many of these are native to the United States.

CLAMS

These bivalves—widely known thanks to spaghetti alle vongole and clam chowder—are farm raised in various locations along the northern coastal areas of the US and Canada, and in Europe. They live just below the surface of the sand.

COCKLES

These delicious little shellfish live in tidal areas and spend a few hours each day above the waterline. The shells are raked out of the sand by hand, using cockle rakes. The flesh inside the shell is firm and sweetish.

MUSSELS

Fresh mussels are in season from late May through February. At the start of the season, we get the longline or rope mussels, which grow on ropes just below the water's surface. These are followed by bottom mussels, which are picked off the seabed as soon as they're ready for consumption.

OYSTERS

Oysters are harvested all over the world and taste different depending on where they're sourced from. They're native to both the East and West coasts of the US, as well as the Gulf of Mexico.

RAZOR CLAMS

These elongated shells, also known as jackknife clams, are found on the North American Atlantic coast, from Canada to South Carolina. Their flavor, briny and sweet, isn't too dissimilar from rounder clams. They are both tasty and easy to prepare.

SCALLOPS

The flesh of these shellfish tastes sweet and has a tender and delicate texture. They are great eaten raw, marinated, or pan-fried. The best sea scallops come from Scandinavia, Scotland, and the US, where they are hand-caught by divers. Bay scallops (such as Nantucket Bay scallops), which are smaller and sweeter than sea scallops, can be found seasonally from late fall through winter.

CRUSTACEANS

Crustaceans, sea-dwelling shellfish with hard exoskeletons, include crayfish, lobsters, and shrimp. Because crustaceans spoil easily, they're best prepared immediately after they're caught, or bought frozen.

CRAB

There are lots of different crab species all over the world and five that are widely consumed in the US. Blue crabs, found in coastal lagoons from Nova Scotia to Uruguay, are the most popular variety on the Eastern Seaboard, where they are often prepared and eaten whole. Dungeness crabs, found on the West Coast of the US, have a sweet, mild, and slightly nutty flavor. King crabs, which can weigh around eleven pounds and achieve a leg span of up to 6 feet (2 m), can found in Alaska. Their sweet leg meat has a flavor reminiscent of lobster. Snow crabs (also known as queen crabs), found from Alaska to Northern Siberia and around the world, have very long legs, which are commonly eaten with melted butter. Stone crabs, primarily found in Florida, are harvested for their right claws, which have a sweet flavor. Harvesters snap off the claw and throw the live crab back into the water, where it will grow a new one.

CRAYFISH

Also known as crawfish, this freshwater variant of the lobster is small and can be bought precooked and frozen. Peeled crayfish are good in salads or as an alternative to lobster in other recipes.

LANGOUSTINE

This slim orange lobster is also known as the Norway lobster. It has a sweet and delicate flavor.

LOBSTER

The American, or Atlantic, lobster is most widely available in the US. When out hunting for food, the lobster uses two claws: the blunter claw for cracking open the carapaces of crabs, the sharper one for cutting and lifting food to its mouth.

PRAWNS & SHRIMP

Prawns and shrimp are found all over the world, in all shapes and sizes. Brown, or gray, shrimp is caught in the North Sea, while the northern prawn is common in the cold waters around Norway and Canada. Larger prawns like the king or tiger prawn are caught in the wild or farmed in tanks, are available in different sizes, and are mostly sold frozen.

CEPHALOPODS

Cephalopods are mollusks, and include octopus, squid, and cuttlefish. To prevent cephalopods from becoming rubbery, cook them either very briefly at a high temperature or very slowly at a low temperature. This is true for both squid and cuttlefish; octopus should always be cooked for a long time at a low heat.

CUTTLEFISH

Cuttlefish have a thicker body than squid. Brief cooking yields extremely tender and somewhat briny flesh. The chalklike skeletons of cuttlefish are often seen on the beach, and are used in bird cages as a calcium supplement for birds. Cuttlefish ink, like squid ink, is used in pasta, rice, and seafood dishes to provide a deep black color and briny flavor.

OCTOPUS

During the day, this mollusk hides among rocks, and at night it goes out hunting. The flesh of its eight limbs is firm and its flavor unique. You can buy octopus whole, but the tentacles, which are often precooked, are also widely available.

SQUID

This species, which has two more limbs than the octopus, lives in shallow and deep sea waters, including off the East and West Coasts of the US. Both the tube (the squid's body) and the tentacles can be eaten.

SUSTAINABLE FISHING

Years ago, I entered the world of fish to find fisheries that set a good example for the future. I loved seafood, but wanted to eat it with a clear conscience, so I looked for fish that was both plentiful and caught in a responsible way. While I was traveling, it also became abundantly clear to me that we have to take good care of our fishing communities. If we value fishermen and treat them well, they, in turn, will look after the sea. But aside from maintaining fish stocks and improving fishing methods, there are other ways we can contribute to better seafood consumption.

In Australia, I had the privilege of meeting Josh Niland, who generously provided an endorsement for this book. In my opinion, he's the most progressive chef on the planet right now. He approaches fish the way a butcher approaches meat. Some of it is dry-aged for up to thirty days, and he uses almost the whole fish. In his master class, which I was fortunate enough to attend in London, he used 96 percent of a sea bass in a range of dishes. By contrast, traditional kitchens only manage to use an average of 50 percent of each individual fish. So many parts are great for cooking, yet they're still thrown away in most cases. As we look toward the future, I hope that Niland will continue to be a huge inspiration for chefs and home cooks alike.

I'm surprised by the number of keen vegetarians who tell me that they'd love to eat fish, but they simply have no confidence in the product. Can we still eat fish? Can we be sure about the provenance? These are the same questions I had fifteen years ago, which prompted me to go in search of people who fish sustainably.

Meanwhile, the world of fish has gradually become more transparent, with the MSC (Marine Stewardship Council) label for wild-caught fish, enabling consumers to make sustainable choices. This label proves the fish is sourced from a healthy fish stock and caught in a selective, responsible way. There's no reason not to eat seafood, as long as you opt for certified products. Likewise, the Monterey Bay Aquarium's Seafood Watch is a handy tool for checking what fish (both farmed and wild) you can and cannot consume responsibly.

I'm also often asked whether we ought to stop eating seafood altogether. Aside from the fact that, from the standpoint of marine biology, this isn't necessary to make the oceans more sustainable, we ought to remember that over two hundred million people depend on fishing for their livelihoods—the majority of them in developing countries.

By using vegetables as the focus of your dishes, you don't have to serve huge portions of fish. I also recommend eating more frozen and canned seafood. Fish is caught during the height of season and then frozen or canned to an increasingly high standard. It's easy to check the packaging to see if the fish has been certified sustainable. So to contribute to the health of the oceans, you don't always need to opt for fresh fish.

HEALTHY EATING

Vegetables and fish are a beautiful match. Not only do their flavors complement each other, but they're both really healthy, too. Fish is pure goodness from the water, and veggies offer goodness from the land. Combine them and you have a perfect meal.

Did you know that fish is good for your heart, blood vessels, and brain? It contains omega-3 fatty acids known as fish oils. If you don't eat fish, it's difficult to get enough of these healthy fats. But there's plenty of them in oily fish such as mackerel, salmon, herring, and sardines. Fish also contains plenty of protein, vitamin B12, vitamin D, and the minerals iodine, phosphorus, and selenium. In other words, there are definite health benefits to eating seafood. It should come as no surprise that the USDA Dietary Guidelines advise us to eat at least 8 ounces (225 g) of seafood per week.

Nutritionists around the world agree that vegetables are the cornerstone of a healthy diet. A generous portion of vegetables adds not only color and flavor to your meals, but also plenty of healthy nutrients like vitamins A and C, folic acid, and the minerals iron, calcium, and potassium. The fact that vegetables contain hardly any calories is an added bonus. By eating them, you look after your immune system, skin, bones, and energy levels. And vegetables are also packed with bioactive compounds like carotenoids and flavonoids, which give them their beautiful hues (they make carrots orange and tomatoes red). But they're more than just natural colorants; as antioxidants, they also protect the cells in your body. And if all that isn't enough, vegetables are high in fiber, too. Fiber is good for your gut and makes you feel full, so you're less likely to feel hungry again soon after eating.

I believe that vegetables are the key to a healthy diet. That said, I couldn't pinpoint a particular vegetable as being the healthiest. Each one is unique and contains a different mix of wholesome nutrients. That's why it's good to eat a wide variety.

For the recipes in this book, I haven't limited myself to vegetables of the land. I also often cook with sea vegetables and seaweeds. The briny flavor of seaweed is somewhat reminiscent of fish and the nutrients are reminiscent of vegetables. Like fish, it's also a good source of iodine and phosphorus. And like vegetables, seaweed contains vitamin C, iron, calcium, potassium, and fiber. No wonder I'm such a big fan. And, if you're not yet, I hope the recipes in this book will convert you.

Healthy and tasty go hand in hand with vegetables and fish. They combine the best of two worlds. And *that's* why I've given both of them a leading role in this book.

MY PANTRY

I always make sure I have a good selection of pantry staples. The quality of these products may vary, but my advice is never to skimp on these essential items. They can make or break your dish.

EGGS
I use medium eggs, and always organic. I store them in their carton in the fridge.

DRIED HERBS & SPICES
Good-quality dried herbs and spices are indispensable in the kitchen. It's handy to have a basic assortment:

Caraway seeds, cardamom, cayenne pepper, cinnamon sticks, cloves, coriander seeds, cumin seeds, fennel seeds, fenugreek, juniper berries, oregano, paprika (sweet and smoked), pink peppercorns, ras el hanout, red pepper flakes, rosemary, dried rose petals, saffron powder, saffron threads, star anise, sumac, thyme, togarashi, turmeric, za'atar.

GHEE & BUTTER
I often cook with ghee (Indian clarified butter). And I always have good-quality butter in my fridge.

OLIVE OIL
I always have light olive oil on hand for frying vegetables and fish. I use extra virgin olive oil for dishes served cold or at room temperature.

PEANUT OIL & SUNFLOWER OIL
I use these mostly for warm preparations because they're suitable for high-heat cooking. I also frequently use coconut, canola, grapeseed, and sesame oils.

PEPPER
I have a pepper mill with black peppercorns and a jar of ground white pepper. White pepper is a bit more subtle, and has an earthy taste. Black pepper is more fiery; too much can be overpowering.

SALT
I use flaky sea salt to finish dishes. Maldon sea salt is my personal favorite, but fleur de sel is good, too. I have a container of fine salt for warm preparations, like boiling vegetables, as well as frying and roasting.

VINEGAR
I love vinegar. The acidity can provide that extra touch to take your dish to the next level. I always have balsamic, red wine, rice, sherry, white, and white wine vinegars in my pantry.

OTHER CONDIMENTS
Tinned or jarred anchovies (salt- or oil-packed), capers (in salt or brine), cognac, Dijon mustard, fish sauce, gherkins (small sour pickles), red and green harissa, grated horseradish, mirin, white miso, pomegranate molasses, light and dark soy sauce, Tabasco sauce, tahini, pure vanilla extract, and Worcestershire sauce.

RAW

Plenty of vegetables and fish can be served raw. When you choose raw, you choose to lock in maximum nutrients, fresh natural flavors, vibrant colors, and beautiful textures. This chapter also features recipes in which the vegetables and fish are not technically raw but have had a cold preparation like a salt marinade, or have been tenderized in pickling liquid. The recipes here all serve two as an appetizer.

TUNA TARTARE
with Frisée Salad

This recipe was inspired by one of my favorite dishes: classic steak tartare, a staple in Parisian bistros. Here, I've replaced the raw beef with fresh tuna fillet, which has a similar meaty texture. Feel free to use a pasteurized egg yolk instead of fresh, or replace the egg with some extra olive oil to give this tartare a smooth, creamy texture. Serve with toasted bread.

SERVES 2
PREPARATION TIME: 20 MINUTES

SALAD
¼ head of frisée
2 teaspoons Dijon mustard
1 tablespoon white wine vinegar
Salt and pepper, to taste
3 tablespoons light olive oil

TUNA TARTARE
1 shallot, minced
4 cornichons (small gherkins), diced
1 scallion, finely chopped
4 flat-leaf parsley sprigs, leaves only, finely chopped
1 tablespoon capers, rinsed, drained, and minced
5½ ounces (160 g) yellowfin tuna fillet, cut into ¼-inch (6 mm) cubes
1 tablespoon plus 1 teaspoon extra virgin olive oil
Hot sauce, such as Tabasco
2 egg yolks
6 chives, finely chopped

To make the salad, trim off the bottom of the frisée, separate the leaves, rinse, and dry well.

Combine the mustard, white wine vinegar, and a pinch of salt in a small bowl. Whisk in the oil, then season with additional salt and pepper. If the dressing is too thick, add a few drops of water. Set aside until you're ready to serve.

To make the tartare, combine the shallot, cornichons, scallion, parsley, and capers in a medium bowl. Add the tuna, the oil, a few drops of hot sauce, salt, and pepper, and mix thoroughly.

To serve, dress the frisée. Serve the salad topped with the tartare and an egg yolk (in the shell, if desired), and scatter the chives over the top.

CALORIES 448 — FAT 39 G — SAT FAT 6 G — CARBS 4 G
SUGAR 1 G — PROTEIN 23 G — SODIUM 351 MG — FIBER 1G

CUCUMBER & FENNEL SALAD
with Gin & Tonic Salmon

In the past, fresh salmon was marinated so it would last longer. These days, we marinate fish to add flavor. Marinating the fish for a maximum of 24 hours allows it to absorb the mild flavors of the gin and tonic.

SERVES 2
MARINATING TIME: 24 HOURS
PREPARATION TIME: 30 MINUTES

MARINATED SALMON
7 ounces (200 g) skin-on salmon fillet
3 black peppercorns
2 juniper berries
1 tablespoon coriander seeds
1 tablespoon fennel seeds
Zest of 1 lemon
2 tablespoons light brown sugar
2 tablespoons coarse sea salt
1 tablespoon gin
1 tablespoon tonic water
Pepper, to taste

DRESSING
Zest and juice of ½ orange
Juice of ½ lime
1 tablespoon extra virgin olive oil
1½ teaspoons grated horseradish
2 teaspoons walnut oil
Salt, to taste

SALAD
⅓ cup (50 g) shelled fresh fava beans
½ cucumber, thinly sliced lengthwise
½ fennel bulb, cored and thinly sliced
3 dill sprigs, leaves only

To marinate the salmon, make cuts in the salmon skin ¾ inch (2 cm) long and ½ inch (13 mm) deep. Line a plate with plastic wrap and place the salmon in it, skin side down.

Crush the peppercorns, juniper berries, coriander seeds, and fennel seeds in a mortar. (The spices don't have to be finely ground; they can retain some of their structure.) Add half of the lemon zest, then mix in the sugar, salt, gin, and tonic water.

Spread the mixture over the salmon and cover it tightly with plastic wrap. Top with a weighted plate or platter, so the flavors can infuse the salmon. Marinate in the fridge for 18 to 24 hours.

Remove the salmon from the fridge and scrape off the marinade. Rinse the fish under gently running cool water and pat dry with a paper towel. Remove the skin with a chef's knife (see page 246). Sprinkle with the remaining lemon zest and some freshly ground pepper. Cut the fish crosswise into ¼-inch (6 mm) strips.

To make the dressing, whisk together the orange zest and juice, lime juice, olive oil, horseradish, and walnut oil. Season with salt and pepper.

To make the salad, blanch the fava beans for 10 to 12 minutes in a pan of gently boiling water with a pinch of salt. Cool in a sieve under cold running water, then slip off the skins.

Toss the cucumber, fennel, and fava beans with the dressing and the dill.

Serve the salad with the salmon strips on top.

> **NOTE:** You can just as easily marinate an entire salmon fillet. Quadruple the other ingredients for a fillet weighing 1¾ to 2¼ pounds (800 g to 1 kg).

CALORIES 324 —— FAT 17 G —— SAT FAT 1 G —— CARBS 21 G
SUGAR 7 G —— PROTEIN 20 G —— SODIUM 651 MG —— FIBER 4 G

NIKKEI OYSTERS, TWO WAYS

Since the late nineteenth century, Peru has been home to many people of Japanese descent. Back then, in Japan, rumor was that there was a lot of gold for the taking in Peru. But the real gold is the fusion of Japanese and Peruvian cuisine: It's known as Nikkei food.

SERVES 2
PREPARATION TIME: 20 MINUTES

12 oysters
1 lime, halved, for serving

SAKE-SOY DRESSING
1 tablespoon soy sauce
1 tablespoon mirin
1 tablespoon sake
1-inch (2.5 cm) piece of cucumber, seeded and diced
½ scallion, thinly sliced
¼-inch (6 mm) piece of ginger, peeled and grated
1 teaspoon toasted sesame oil
1 tablespoon tobiko (flying fish roe)

JALAPEÑO-LIME DRESSING
½ jalapeño, seeded and minced
½ shallot, finely chopped
Juice of 1 lime
1 teaspoon sesame oil
2 cilantro sprigs, leaves only, finely chopped

Open the oysters (see page 240). Strain the oyster liquor through a fine sieve and set aside.

To make the sake-soy dressing, mix the soy sauce, mirin, sake, and 1 tablespoon of the oyster liquor in another small bowl. Pour this over half of the oysters.

Mix the cucumber, scallion, and ginger in another small bowl. Scatter the mixture over the dressed oysters, then drizzle with the sesame oil. Top with the tobiko.

To make the jalapeño-lime dressing, mix the jalapeño, shallot, and lime juice in a small bowl. Stir in 1½ teaspoons of the remaining oyster liquor and the sesame oil. Pour this over the second bowl of oysters, mix, and garnish with the cilantro.

Serve each bowl of oysters with a lime half.

CALORIES 331 —— FAT 12 G —— SAT FAT 2 G —— CARBS 22 G
SUGAR 3 G —— PROTEIN 31 G —— SODIUM 851 MG —— FIBER 0 G

VEGETABLE CEVICHE
with Hake & Jalapeño Tiger's Milk

Ever since my first trip to Peru several years ago, ceviche has been a favorite of mine. It offers endless possibilities for both fish and vegetables. The ingredients are marinated, or cured, in what is known as "tiger's milk," a spicy citrus marinade. Usually including lime but containing no actual milk or tigers, it's the cornerstone of every ceviche. This recipe also works well with other white fish, such as cod, haddock, or pollock. Leftover jalapeño paste will keep for a week in the fridge or up to 6 months in the freezer.

SERVES 2
PREPARATION TIME: 30 MINUTES

JALAPEÑO PASTE
3 jalapeños, seeded
1 tablespoon chopped onion
1 garlic clove, coarsely chopped
2 tablespoons extra virgin olive oil

CEVICHE
1 small sweet potato (about 7 ounces/200 g)
2 teaspoons jalapeño paste
Juice of 2 limes
½ teaspoon salt
5 ounces (140 g) hake fillet, cut into ¾-inch (2 cm) slices
1 to 2 teaspoons Fish Stock (page 232; optional)
1 avocado, pitted, peeled, and chopped
½ red onion, sliced into rings
1 tablespoon pomegranate seeds
3 cilantro sprigs, leaves only

To make the jalapeño paste, blend the jalapeños, onion, garlic, and oil in a blender or food processor until smooth. Set aside in a covered container.

To make the ceviche, bring a small pot of water with a pinch of salt to a boil. Cook the sweet potato until fork-tender, 15 to 20 minutes. Remove the skin and let the flesh cool, then cut into ¾-inch (2 cm) cubes.

Whisk together 2 teaspoons of the jalapeño paste, the lime juice, and the salt in a medium bowl. Add the fish and stir to combine. If you'd like to reduce the acidity, add the fish stock. Let rest for 5 minutes to allow the fish to cure.

Gently fold in the avocado, sweet potato, and onion, reserving some for garnish.

Serve with the reserved avocado, sweet potato, and onion on top, along with a sprinkle of pomegranate seeds and cilantro leaves.

CALORIES 349 —— FAT 18 G —— SAT FAT 3 G —— CARBS 33 G
SUGAR 9 G —— PROTEIN 17 G —— SODIUM 652 MG —— FIBER 8 G

RAW BEETS
with Boquerones & Manchego

Boquerones are the number one tapas dish in Spain. They're made by marinating raw anchovy fillets in white wine vinegar for a few hours. Here, the earthy notes of the wafer-thin beets and the salty Manchego cheese are a perfect match for the briny anchovy. No time to marinate your own boquerones? You can buy them ready to eat. You can also use sardine fillets for this recipe.

SERVES 2
MARINATING TIME: 6 HOURS
PREPARATION TIME: 15 MINUTES

BOQUERONES
3 to 4 ounces (100 g) fresh
 anchovy fillets
1 teaspoon salt
⅓ cup (80 ml) white wine vinegar
2 garlic cloves, peeled
2 tablespoons extra virgin olive oil
1 flat-leaf parsley sprig, leaves only,
 finely chopped

7 ounces (200 g) mixed beets (red,
 Chioggia, yellow), peeled and
 thinly sliced
Extra virgin olive oil
Juice of ½ lemon
Flaky sea salt and pepper, to taste
1¾ ounces (50 g) Manchego, thinly
 sliced

To make the boquerones, place the anchovy fillets on a plate, skin side up. Sprinkle with ½ teaspoon of the salt and pour the vinegar on top until they are just covered. Cover and marinate in the fridge for 5 hours.

Remove the anchovies from the marinade and briefly rinse under cold running water. Pat dry with a paper towel and place them side by side on a platter. Coarsely chop 1 of the garlic cloves, then pound it with the remaining ½ teaspoon salt in a mortar to form a paste. Stir in 2 tablespoons olive oil, then pour the mixture over the anchovy fillets. Cover and marinate in the fridge for about 1 hour.

Take the anchovies out of the fridge 15 minutes before serving to bring them up to room temperature. Finely chop the remaining garlic clove, then sprinkle it over the anchovies along with the parsley.

Toss the beets with ¼ cup (60 ml) olive oil and let rest for 6 to 8 minutes. Add the lemon juice and gently combine, then season with salt and pepper. Top the beets with the boquerones and cheese and serve.

CALORIES 515 —— FAT 46 G —— SAT FAT 12 G —— CARBS 9 G
SUGARS 5 G —— PROTEIN 18 G —— SODIUM 849 MG —— FIBER 2 G

WATERCRESS & CILANTRO SALSA VERDE
with Swordfish & Tomato

This is my take on a classic salsa verde, a green herb sauce. This salsa pairs terrifically well with raw fish. The peppery notes of the watercress add a bit of punch to the salsa. But feel free to use other herbs, including basil, parsley, chervil, or dill.

SERVES 2
PREPARATION TIME: 20 MINUTES

SALSA VERDE
10 watercress sprigs, leaves only
6 cilantro sprigs, leaves only
Generous ⅓ cup (90 ml) light olive oil
2 tablespoons red wine vinegar
2 teaspoons capers, rinsed and drained
Juice of ¼ lemon
½ garlic clove
Salt and pepper, to taste

7 ounces (200 g) swordfish steak, skin removed
Extra virgin olive oil
Handful of mixed salad greens of your choice
6 cherry tomatoes, quartered
1 scallion, thinly sliced
10 pea shoots or other sprouted beans
2 tablespoons sliced almonds
2 teaspoons capers, rinsed and drained
½ Preserved Lemon (page 237), rind only, thinly sliced

To make the salsa, blend the watercress, cilantro, oil, vinegar, capers, lemon juice, and garlic in a blender or food processor until smooth. Season with salt and pepper and set aside.

Lay the swordfish on a cutting board. Place one hand on the fish and, using a fillet knife or other thin, sharp knife, slice it horizontally as thinly as possible. Wrap each slice in a piece of plastic wrap or parchment paper. Pound the slices with a meat tenderizer or the bottom of a saucepan to further flatten them, until they are no more than 1 to 2 millimeters thick.

Lightly coat two plates with olive oil to prevent the fish from sticking. Divide the swordfish between the plates.

Dollop a tablespoon of salsa verde on top of the swordfish on each plate. Toss the greens and tomatoes with a bit of olive oil in a small bowl to coat them lightly. Heap them on top of the salsa verde and fish.

Scatter the scallion, pea shoots, almonds, capers, and preserved lemon over the plates. Serve the remaining salsa verde on the side.

CALORIES 485 —— FAT 44 G —— SAT FAT 1 G —— CARBS 9 G
SUGARS 3 G —— PROTEIN 20 G —— SODIUM 683 MG —— FIBER 3 G

SALMON TATAKI SALAD
with Miso Dressing

Tataki is a classic Japanese style of preparing fish. It involves briefly searing the outside to give it a crispy coating and a pleasant bitterness. You can add extra flavor by first dipping the fish in sesame seeds and dried spices. Make sure to cool the fish immediately after frying so the inside remains raw. Use tuna instead of salmon, if you prefer.

SERVES 2
PREPARATION TIME: 25 MINUTES

MISO DRESSING
2 tablespoons canola oil
2 tablespoons sesame oil
2 tablespoons rice vinegar
1 tablespoon mirin
1 tablespoon soy sauce
Juice of ½ lime
1 tablespoon white miso

SALAD
3 tablespoons white sesame seeds
2 tablespoons black sesame seeds
Oil, for frying
1 teaspoon coriander seeds, crushed
7 ounces (200 g) skinless salmon fillet, cut into large chunks
½ cucumber, seeded and cut into long strips
2 medium carrots, peeled and cut into thin strips
2 scallions, sliced
4 radishes, sliced
3 tablespoons shelled cooked soybeans (edamame)
1 tablespoon daikon radish microgreens (optional)

To make the dressing, mix the canola oil, sesame oil, rice vinegar, mirin, soy sauce, and lime juice. Whisk in the miso until smooth.

To make the salad, toast 1 tablespoon of the white sesame seeds in a dry frying pan over medium heat, stirring constantly, until golden brown, 2 to 3 minutes. Transfer to a plate to cool.

Mix the remaining 2 tablespoons white sesame seeds with the black sesame seeds and coriander seeds on a plate. Brush the pieces of salmon lightly with oil all over, then dredge them in the sesame and coriander mixture. Make sure all sides are properly coated.

Heat a dry frying pan over high heat. Sear the salmon for about 30 seconds on each side until the coating is slightly caramelized.

Remove the fish from the pan and immediately cut into ½-inch (13 mm) slices, to stop the cooking process.

Toss the cucumber, carrot, scallion, radish, and soybeans with half of the dressing and toasted white sesame seeds in a medium bowl. Top the salad with the salmon and garnish with radish greens (if using). Serve the remaining dressing on the side.

CALORIES 661 —— FAT 45 G —— SAT FAT 6 G —— CARBS 17 G
SUGARS 9 G —— PROTEIN 25 G —— SODIUM 991 MG —— FIBER 4 G

MACKEREL POKE BOWL

The poke bowl, which originated in Hawaii, has taken the rest of the Western world by storm in recent years. This one combines the crunch of vegetables and the tender texture of oily fish with sweet-and-sour sushi rice. Cut the mackerel fillets crosswise into pretty slices, like they do in Hawaii (poke means "to slice").

SERVES 2
PREPARATION TIME: 45 MINUTES

RICE
½ cup (125 g) sushi rice
3 tablespoons rice vinegar
½ teaspoon salt
½ teaspoon sugar

DRESSING
1 tablespoon sesame oil
1 tablespoon soy sauce
1 tablespoon mirin
1 tablespoon rice vinegar

4 ounces (120 g) mackerel fillet, skinned, sliced crosswise
½ cup (50 g) cooked shelled soybeans (edamame)
¾ ounce (20 g) chuka wakame (Japanese seaweed salad)
1 avocado, pitted, peeled, and sliced
½ cucumber, seeded and cut into long strips
1 carrot, peeled and grated
5 radishes, sliced
3 tablespoons salmon roe

To prepare the rice, rinse it in a sieve under running water until the water runs clear. Drain well. Transfer the rice to a saucepan and add water until the rice is covered and the water comes up to your second knuckle. Bring to a boil, cover, and simmer for 15 minutes, until the rice is just tender. Remove from the heat and let stand, covered, for 15 minutes more.

Meanwhile, heat the vinegar, sugar, and salt in a small saucepan. Stir until the sugar dissolves; let cool.

When the rice is lukewarm, add the vinegar mixture and toss to mix well. Spread the rice on a plate and let cool.

To make the dressing, whisk together the sesame oil, soy sauce, mirin, and rice vinegar in a small bowl.

Serve the rice in bowls, topped with the mackerel, soybeans, wakame, avocado, cucumber, carrot, radish, and salmon roe. Serve the dressing on the side.

CALORIES 673 —— FAT 35 G —— SAT FAT 6 G —— CARBS 63 G
SUGARS 10 G —— PROTEIN 28 G —— SODIUM 1,226 MG —— FIBER 9 G

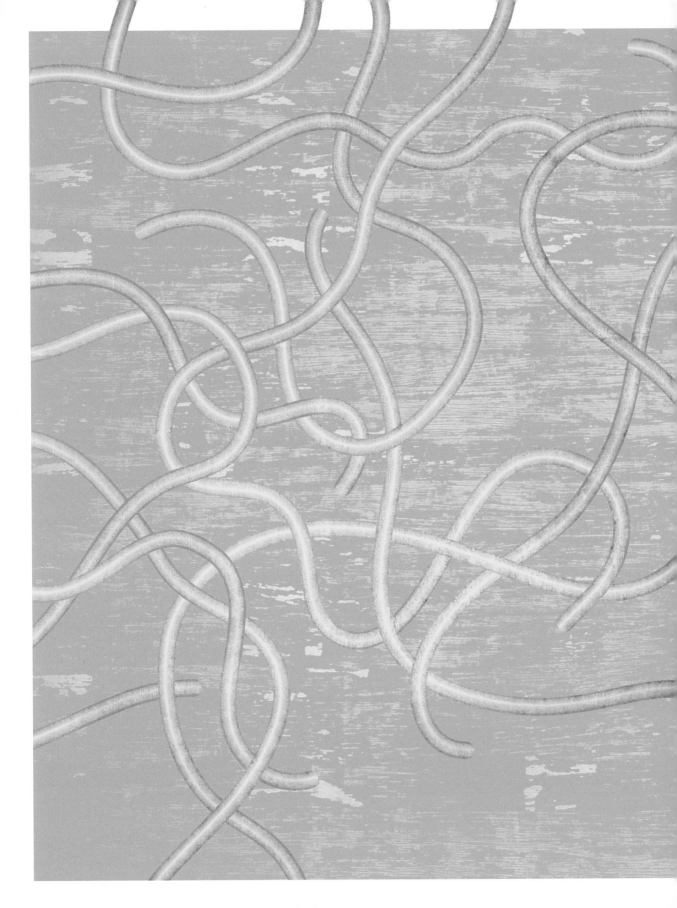

SOUPS

CAULIFLOWER SOUP
WITH CRAB & TARRAGON OIL — 53

POTATO & WATERCRESS SOUP
WITH HOT-SMOKED HERRING — 54

MISO RAMEN
WITH VEGETABLES &
SCALLOPS — 57

TOMATO & SHRIMP GAZPACHO — 58

LAKSA
WITH SUGAR SNAP PEAS,
PRAWNS & CLAMS — 61

CUCUMBER SOUP
WITH SEA BASS TARTARE — 62

This chapter doesn't feature any traditional fish soups. Instead, it contains big, flavorful vegetable soups—with fish as a tasty complement. They range from refreshing summer soups to hearty winter fare. Most of them are made with vegetable stock, but feel free to experiment with fish or shellfish stocks.

CAULIFLOWER SOUP
with Crab & Tarragon Oil

Cauliflower pairs really well with the sweet flavor of crab. You can use any kind of crab in this recipe. I use king crab, made famous by the reality TV show *Deadliest Catch,* about crab fishing in the Bering Sea off Alaska. Serve with good crusty bread.

SERVES 2
PREPARATION TIME: 30 MINUTES

SOUP

2 tablespoons extra virgin olive oil
1 onion, diced
1 leek, white and light green parts only, thinly sliced
7 ounces (200 g) starchy potatoes, peeled and diced
1 small head of cauliflower (about 12 ounces/340 g), separated into florets
3 cups (720 ml) Vegetable Stock (page 232)
2 tarragon sprigs, leaves only, coarsely chopped, plus extra whole leaves
Salt and pepper, to taste
10 ounces (285 g) king or snow crab legs, cooked

TARRAGON OIL

4 tarragon sprigs, leaves only
3 tablespoons extra virgin olive oil
½ teaspoon fresh lemon juice

Preheat the oven to 325°F (165°C).

To make the soup, heat 2 tablespoons oil in a large pot over medium heat. Sauté the onion and leek until soft, 3 to 4 minutes. Add the potato and cauliflower and sauté for 1 minute.

Pour in the vegetable stock and bring to a boil. Simmer until the potato and cauliflower are tender, about 15 minutes. Remove from the heat and purée the soup with an immersion blender, or transfer, in batches, to a blender and purée. Stir in the chopped tarragon and season with salt and pepper. Keep the soup warm.

Meanwhile, prepare the tarragon oil by pounding the tarragon leaves in a mortar with a generous pinch of salt. Mix in the olive oil and season with the lemon juice and pepper. Strain the oil through a fine sieve and discard the solids.

Crack the crab legs (you can leave the shells on, but cracking them will make things easier when you eat the soup) and warm them in the oven for 3 to 4 minutes, until lukewarm.

Serve the crab legs in the soup and garnish with a few extra tarragon leaves. Serve the tarragon oil on the side.

CALORIES 384 —— FAT 15 G —— SAT FAT 2 G —— CARBS 30 G
SUGARS 13 G —— PROTEIN 32 G —— SODIUM 1,296 MG —— FIBER 10 G

POTATO & WATERCRESS SOUP
with Hot-Smoked Herring

This recipe calls for buckling, which are whole, hot-smoked herrings. Their smoky flavor is a perfect match for the creamy soup. If you can't find buckling, you can use hot-smoked salmon or smoked trout instead. Vichyssoise, as this soup is also known, is traditionally served cold, but it's also very good warm.

SERVES 2
PREPARATION TIME: 40 MINUTES

1 tablespoon butter
1 leek, white and light green parts only, thinly sliced
1 shallot, finely chopped
1 garlic clove, minced
2 tablespoons white wine
10 ounces (285 g) starchy potatoes, peeled and cut into ¾-inch (2 cm) cubes
Generous 2 cups (500 ml) Vegetable Stock (page 232)
¼ cup (60 ml) light cream
1½ cups (60 g) watercress, leaves only
¼ teaspoon grated nutmeg
Salt and pepper, to taste
2 buckling (about 2.5 ounces/70 g each), filleted
2 chervil sprigs, leaves only
Extra virgin olive oil

Preheat the oven to 200°F (90°C).

Melt the butter in a large pot over medium heat. Add the leek, shallot, and garlic. Cook, stirring, for 1 to 2 minutes, until slightly softened, before adding the wine. Reduce the heat, cover, and braise the vegetables for 10 minutes, until tender. Don't let the vegetables brown.

Rinse the potatoes under cold running water to remove some of the starch, then add to the pot. Immediately add the stock and bring to a boil. Reduce the heat and simmer uncovered until the potatoes are tender, about 15 minutes.

Pour in the cream and cook for 5 minutes more. Add most of the watercress (save some for garnish) and the nutmeg, then turn off the heat. Purée the soup with an immersion blender, or transfer, in batches, to a blender and purée. Season with salt and pepper. Keep warm.

Place the buckling on a baking sheet and warm in the oven for 6 to 8 minutes. Break the fish into large pieces.

Serve the soup garnished with the buckling, reserved watercress, and the chervil. Drizzle olive oil over the top.

CALORIES 277 — FAT 15 G — SAT FAT 7 G — CARBS 19 G
SUGARS 5 G — PROTEIN 16 G — SODIUM 1,163 MG — FIBER 5 G

MISO RAMEN
with Vegetables & Scallops

Miso ramen is so delicious. This famous Japanese noodle soup is the ideal vehicle for a vegetable-and-fish combo. It's usually made with fish or shellfish stock, but you can also use half fish and half vegetable stock. Don't overcook the vegetables; they should retain their crunch. This soup is fantastic served with velvety seared scallops.

SERVES 2
PREPARATION TIME: 30 MINUTES

1¼ cups (300 ml) Fish Stock (page 232)
1¼ cups (300 ml) Vegetable Stock (page 232)
1 tablespoon white miso
1 egg
Salt and pepper, to taste
Oil, for cooking
7 ounces (200 g) ramen or rice noodles
2 ounces (60 g) shiitake mushrooms, stems removed, coarsely chopped
1 head of bok choy, root end trimmed, coarsely chopped
¼ head of napa cabbage, sliced crosswise
2 tablespoons soy sauce
2 teaspoons mirin
6 scallops, side muscle removed, patted dry
1 scallion, finely chopped
¼ cup (40 g) bean sprouts
Handful of alfalfa sprouts
2 cilantro sprigs

Whisk the fish and vegetable stocks and miso together in a saucepan and warm over low heat. Make sure the stock doesn't come to a boil.

Beat the egg in a small bowl and season with salt. Heat a splash of oil in a small frying pan over medium heat. Pour in the egg and let cook for 2 to 3 minutes, flipping halfway through, until softly cooked through. Remove from the pan and cut into thin strips. Set aside.

Bring a large pot of water to a boil and cook the noodles according to package directions. Drain, then rinse under cold water to prevent them from sticking. Drain again well.

Heat 1 tablespoon oil in a large frying pan or wok over medium-high heat. Sauté the mushrooms for 1 to 2 minutes, until lightly darkened. Add the bok choy and cabbage and stir-fry for 1 minute, until slightly caramelized.

Add the soy sauce and mirin, and season with pepper. Mix in the noodles until heated through, then divide the noodle-vegetable mixture between two soup bowls. Pour in the stock mixture until the noodles are almost but not completely covered. Keep warm.

Clean the frying pan and heat 1 tablespoon oil over medium-high heat. Season both sides of the scallops with salt. Once the oil is hot, sear the scallops for about 1 minute on each side.

Top the noodles and vegetables with scallops and egg strips. Scatter the scallion, bean sprouts, and alfalfa sprouts on top, and garnish with the cilantro.

CALORIES 692 —— FAT 21 G —— SAT FAT 2 G —— CARBS 102 G
SUGARS 9 G —— PROTEIN 26 G —— SODIUM 1,790 MG —— FIBER 7 G

TOMATO & SHRIMP GAZPACHO

Gazpacho can be made with all kinds of vegetables. This version uses tomato and bell pepper. The binding agent is crucial, as you don't want to end up with regular tomato soup. In Catalonia, Spain, they use white bread soaked in water. This vegetable soup is best served ice-cold.

SERVES 2
PREPARATION TIME: 60 MINUTES

4 large tomatoes, chopped (about 1½ cups/250 g)
1 red bell pepper, seeded and coarsely chopped
½ red onion, coarsely chopped
1 red chile, seeded and coarsely chopped
1 garlic clove, halved
4 basil sprigs, leaves only
3 slices crusty white bread (preferably rustic)
3 tablespoons light olive oil, plus extra for the croutons
1 tablespoon sherry vinegar (optional)
½ teaspoon ground cumin
Salt and pepper, to taste
5 ounces (150 g) cooked, peeled, and deveined small shrimp

In a food processor, blend the tomatoes, pepper, onion, chile, garlic, and basil until smooth.

Remove the crusts from 2 slices of bread and tear the bread into chunks. Soak them under cold running water until saturated. Squeeze out the water with your hands, then add the pulp to the mixture in the food processor. Add the olive oil, vinegar (if using), and cumin, and blend until smooth. Season with salt and pepper.

Transfer the soup to a covered container and refrigerate until thoroughly chilled, at least 30 minutes.

Meanwhile, preheat the oven to 350°F (180°C). Line a baking sheet with parchment paper.

Cut the third slice of bread into large pieces. Toss with about 1 tablespoon of olive oil and a little salt. Place the bread on the baking sheet. Bake the croutons until they're golden brown and crisp, around 10 minutes. Let cool.

Taste the soup and season again with salt and pepper. Serve the gazpacho topped with the shrimp and croutons.

CALORIES 457 —— FAT 25 G —— SAT FAT 1 G —— CARBS 41 G
SUGARS 12 G —— PROTEIN 22 G —— SODIUM 447 MG —— FIBER 6 G

LAKSA
with Sugar Snap Peas, Prawns & Clams

Laksa is the national dish of Malaysia and Singapore. There are lots of different versions of it, some with fish or meat, some completely vegetarian. My take on this creamy coconut noodle soup contains crunchy vegetables, tiger prawns, and clams. The curry paste adds a fiery note, and it's easy to make at home. Store leftover curry paste, well covered, in the fridge for up to 2 weeks.

SERVES 2
PREPARATION TIME: 40 MINUTES

CURRY PASTE
1 teaspoon terasi (shrimp paste)
1 teaspoon cumin seeds
1 teaspoon coriander seeds
3 red chiles, seeded and coarsely chopped
2 shallots, coarsely chopped
3 garlic cloves, coarsely chopped
¾-inch (2 cm) piece of ginger, peeled and coarsely chopped
2 teaspoons ground turmeric, or ¾-inch (2 cm) piece of fresh turmeric, peeled and coarsely chopped
Zest and juice of 1 lime
2 tablespoons sesame oil

8 ounces (230 g) rice noodles

LAKSA
Oil, for frying
6 tiger prawns, peeled and deveined
Salt, to taste
Generous ¾ cup (200 g) coconut milk
1¾ cups (400 ml) Fish Stock (page 232)
About 2 ounces (50 g) sugar snap peas, strings removed
2 green asparagus spears, woody ends removed, halved lengthwise and chopped
2 lemongrass stalks, white part only, bruised

1 teaspoon sugar
2 teaspoons fish sauce
7 ounces (200 g) clams, scrubbed clean
1 scallion, sliced
2 cilantro sprigs
2 lime wedges

To make the curry paste, roast the terasi in a dry frying pan for 2 minutes, until the paste becomes loose and smoky. Transfer to a mortar and let cool.

Crush the cumin and coriander seeds with the terasi. Combine with the chiles, shallots, garlic, ginger, turmeric, lime zest and juice, and sesame oil in the mortar or in a food processor and pound or blend until smooth.

Bring a pot of water to a boil. Cook the noodles according to package directions, drain, then rinse with water to prevent them from sticking. Set aside to drain again.

To make the laksa, heat 2 tablespoons oil in a frying pan over medium heat. Sprinkle the prawns with salt and stir-fry for 2 to 3 minutes, until golden brown. Remove from the pan and set aside.

Fry 2 tablespoons of the curry paste in a dry large saucepan for 2 minutes, until fragrant. Stir in the coconut milk until completely combined. Add the fish stock, sugar snap peas, asparagus, lemongrass, sugar, fish sauce, and clams. Simmer over low heat until the clams open, 4 to 5 minutes. Add the prawns and warm through.

Divide the noodles between two bowls and top with the vegetables and seafood. Pour in the liquid. Serve with scallion, cilantro, and lime wedges.

CALORIES 897 —— FAT 36 G —— SAT FAT 18 G —— CARBS 113 G
SUGARS 7 G —— PROTEIN 32 G —— SODIUM 924 MG —— FIBER 4 G

CUCUMBER SOUP
with Sea Bass Tartare

Cucumber is nice and refreshing, but also a bit neutral in flavor. Combined with this spicy sea bass tartare, however, it makes a delicious cold soup. A perfect summer dish.

SERVES 2
PREPARATION TIME: 40 MINUTES

SOUP

1 cucumber, coarsely chopped
½-inch (13 mm) piece of ginger, peeled and grated
½ garlic clove, minced
2 dill sprigs, leaves only
¼ cup (60 ml) light cream
1 tablespoon fresh lemon juice
Salt and white pepper, to taste
1 cilantro sprig, leaves only
Extra virgin olive oil

TARTARE

3 to 4 ounces (100 g) sea bass fillet, skin removed, diced
¼ medium tomato, seeded and finely chopped (I used green tomato)
¼ scallion, finely chopped
¼ shallot, finely chopped
¼ jalapeño, seeded and finely chopped
2 cilantro sprigs, leaves only, finely chopped
1 teaspoon light olive oil
Juice of ¼ lime

To make the soup, purée the cucumber, ginger, garlic, dill, and cream with an immersion blender until smooth. Season with lemon juice, salt, and pepper. Chill in the refrigerator for 30 minutes.

To make the tartare, combine the sea bass, tomato, scallion, shallot, jalapeño, cilantro, light olive oil, and lime juice. Season with salt.

Pour the soup into two bowls, top with the tartare, and garnish with cilantro and a drizzle of extra virgin olive oil.

CALORIES 166 — FAT 10 G — SAT FAT 4 G — CARBS 8 G
SUGARS 4 G — PROTEIN 13 G — SODIUM 57 MG — FIBER 2 G

SALADS

SALADE LYONNAISE
WITH MOJAMA & ALMONDS — 67

LENTIL SALAD
WITH SMOKED WILD SALMON &
ARUGULA PESTO — 68

WATERMELON SALAD
WITH CRAB & TARRAGON
YOGURT — 71

CAESAR SALAD
WITH ANCHOVIES & TONNATO
DRESSING — 72

POTATO SALAD
WITH HERRING &
ZA'ATAR YOGURT — 76

THAI SALAD
WITH SPICY CALAMARI — 78

POTATO SALAD
WITH TURNIP GREENS & HOT-
SMOKED SALMON — 81

PEAR & FIG SALAD
WITH COD LIVER & ORANGE
DRESSING — 82

You can use pretty much any combination of vegetables for a salad, but most fruits are surprisingly good, too. Smoked and marinated fish, as well as tinned fish, are easy and tasty additions, as is seafood prepared à la minute—that is, prepared right before you're ready to serve. In this chapter, you'll find my own creations as well as some twists on well-known classics.

SALADE LYONNAISE
with Mojama & Almonds

Salade Lyonnaise is a staple on the menus of the famous bouchons in Lyon, France. Traditionally, this salad is made with frisée dressed in a warm vinaigrette and topped with crispy bacon and poached eggs. Here, I've replaced the bacon with mojama, a salt-cured tuna that's laid out to dry in the sun and sea breeze for several weeks. In Andalusia, Spain, where this specialty originates, mojama is also known as pata negra de la mar (pata negra, of course, refers to Iberian pigs, used for the famous jamón Iberico). Mojama is available online, but smoked salmon is a good substitute.

SERVES 2
PREPARATION TIME: 30 MINUTES

CROUTONS
2 slices of bread
1 garlic clove, halved
Extra virgin olive oil

VINAIGRETTE
2 teaspoons Dijon mustard
2 tablespoons sherry vinegar
Generous ⅓ cup (90 ml) extra virgin olive oil
Salt and pepper, to taste

⅓ cup (50 g) blanched raw almonds
½ teaspoon white vinegar
2 eggs (see Tip)
The core of a head of frisée
5 ounces (150 g) mojama (sun-dried tuna), thinly sliced

> **TIP**: The fresher the eggs, the better they will poach.

Preheat the oven to 350°F (180°C). Line a baking sheet with parchment paper.

To make the croutons, rub the bread with the garlic clove. Drizzle the slices with olive oil and cut them into ¾-inch (2 cm) chunks. Place the bread on the baking sheet and bake for 7 to 10 minutes, flipping the pieces after about 4 minutes, until golden brown and crunchy. Let the croutons cool.

Meanwhile, prepare the vinaigrette by whisking together the mustard, sherry vinegar, and a pinch of salt. Add the oil in a slow trickle while continuously whisking to achieve a smooth, well-incorporated dressing. Season with salt and pepper. Whisk in a few drops of water if you prefer a slightly runnier vinaigrette.

Heat a splash of oil in a frying pan over medium-high heat. Toast the almonds until golden brown, 2 to 3 minutes, tossing occasionally. Transfer to a plate and let cool.

Bring a small saucepan of water to a boil and add the white vinegar. Lower the heat so the water is just below a boil. Carefully break an egg into the pan and poach until the white has solidified but the yolk is still runny, 3 minutes. Scoop it out with a skimmer and drain on a kitchen towel. Repeat with the second egg.

Separate the frisée leaves and tear them into large pieces. Toss with the almonds and vinaigrette in a medium bowl. Arrange the salad on plates and top with the mojama slices. Add an egg to each plate and pierce it with a fork to let some of the yolk run out. Scatter the croutons on top and serve immediately.

CALORIES 850 —— FAT 65 G —— SAT FAT 10 G —— CARBS 26 G
SUGARS 4 G —— PROTEIN 48 G —— SODIUM 1385 MG —— FIBER 7 G

LENTIL SALAD
with Smoked Wild Salmon & Arugula Pesto

It was during my first trip to Alaska, many years ago, that I discovered the flavor of genuine smoked wild sockeye. Sockeye salmon feeds on plankton covered in miniature shellfish, which is how it gets its intense red hue. With its soft, almost creamy texture, it's the perfect salmon for a lentil salad with arugula pesto.

SERVES 2
PREPARATION TIME: 45 MINUTES

¾ cup (150 g) Puy lentils
6 flat-leaf parsley sprigs, stems and leaves separated, coarsely chopped
1 bay leaf
1 thyme sprig

PESTO
1 garlic clove, peeled
Salt
2½ cups (50 g) arugula
⅓ cup (30 g) grated Parmesan
¼ cup (30 g) pine nuts
⅓ cup (80 ml) extra virgin olive oil
Fresh lemon juice (optional)

1 tablespoon extra virgin olive oil
2 to 3 ounces (75 g) green beans, trimmed
2 to 3 ounces (75 g) wax beans, trimmed
1 artichoke heart (from a jar, or home-cooked fresh), chopped into pieces
Handful of arugula leaves
3 to 4 ounces (100 g) cold-smoked wild sockeye salmon, sliced

Place a medium saucepan of water over medium-high heat and add the lentils, parsley stems, bay leaf, and thyme. Bring to a boil, lower the heat, and cook the lentils until just tender, about 20 minutes. Drain, remove the bay leaf and thyme, mix in the olive oil, and let cool until lukewarm.

To make the pesto, grind the garlic with a pinch of salt in a food processor to a coarse paste. Add the arugula, cheese, and pine nuts, and pulse briefly. Add the olive oil and continue to pulse until the pesto reaches the desired consistency. Taste and season with lemon juice (if desired). Set aside.

Bring a small saucepan of salted water to a boil. Cook the green and wax beans until fork-tender, 5 to 7 minutes. Drain, then run under cold water to stop the cooking process. Pat dry with a kitchen towel.

Combine the lentils with the beans and artichoke in a medium bowl. Add 2 tablespoons of the pesto and mix thoroughly with your hands. Fold in the arugula, smoked salmon, and most of the parsley leaves.

Serve the salad on a platter, topped with the remaining parsley leaves and the rest of the pesto on the side.

CALORIES 491 — FAT 19 G — SAT FAT 3 G — CARBS 46 G
SUGARS 5 G — PROTEIN 31 G — SODIUM 1,142 MG — FIBER 11 G

WATERMELON SALAD
with Crab & Tarragon Yogurt

A gorgeous summer salad with both vegetables *and* fruit. The sweet flavor of crabmeat pairs terrifically with the refreshing watermelon, which is lightly grilled. The crisp acidity of the Granny Smith apple and tarragon yogurt add a pleasant contrast.

SERVES 2
PREPARATION TIME: 20 MINUTES

TARRAGON YOGURT
¼ cup (60 g) plain Greek yogurt
6 tarragon sprigs, leaves only, chopped
1 tablespoon plus 1 teaspoon extra virgin olive oil
Juice of ¼ lemon
Salt and pepper, to taste

½ small (about 25 ounces/700 g) watermelon, sliced
Extra virgin olive oil
1 small carrot, peeled
1 small turnip, peeled
1 Granny Smith apple, cored and thinly sliced
5 to 6 ounces (160 g) cooked crabmeat
1 small cup (40 g) lamb's lettuce (mâche) or other small-leaf lettuce
1 tablespoon raw, unsalted pistachios, coarsely chopped

To make the tarragon yogurt, mix the yogurt with the tarragon and olive oil. Season with the lemon juice, salt, and pepper. Set aside.

Heat a grill pan over high heat. Brush the watermelon slices with olive oil and grill for 4 to 5 minutes on each side, until the melon is streaked with grill marks. Remove from the pan and cut into triangles.

Thinly slice the carrot and turnip using a mandoline or vegetable peeler.

Arrange the watermelon, carrot, turnip, and apple on a plate. Scatter the crab and lettuce on top and sprinkle with pistachios. Grind some pepper on top and drizzle with olive oil

Serve the salad with the tarragon yogurt on the side.

CALORIES 415 —— FAT 22 G —— SAT FAT 4 G —— CARBS 36 G
SUGARS 28 G —— PROTEIN 22 G —— SODIUM 287 MG —— FIBER 5 G

CAESAR SALAD
with Anchovies & Tonnato Dressing

A Caesar salad with a dressing inspired by vitello tonnato, the Italian classic surf-and-turf dish of tuna and veal. Pistachios and wafer-thin croutons add a bit of crunch. Leftover dressing will keep, covered, in the fridge for several days.

SERVES 2
PREPARATION TIME: 25 MINUTES

10 wafer-thin baguette slices
8 green asparagus tips

DRESSING
One 5-ounce (142 g) can of tuna in
  water, drained
2 oil-packed anchovy fillets,
  drained
3 tablespoons mayonnaise
1 tablespoon capers, rinsed and
  drained
1 teaspoon balsamic vinegar
2 flat-leaf parsley sprigs, leaves
  only
Juice of ¼ lemon
Salt and pepper, to taste

½ head of romaine lettuce, leaves
  separated and coarsely chopped
8 oil-packed anchovy fillets,
  drained
1 tablespoon raw, unsalted
  pistachios, chopped
¼ cup (20 g) shaved Parmesan

Preheat the oven to 350°F (180°C).

Arrange the baguette slices on a rack over a baking sheet and bake for 3 to 5 minutes, until golden brown. Set the croutons aside to cool.

Bring a small saucepan of salted water to a boil. Blanch the asparagus tips until tender-crisp, 2 to 3 minutes. Drain, then run under cold water to stop the cooking process. Pat dry with a kitchen towel.

To make the dressing, blend the tuna, anchovies, mayonnaise, capers, vinegar, and parsley with an immersion blender or in a food processor until smooth. Season with lemon juice and freshly ground pepper. Add salt to taste, but be careful, as the anchovies are already quite salty.

In a medium bowl, toss the romaine and asparagus tips with enough of the dressing to coat them lightly. Arrange the dressed salad on two plates and divide the anchovy fillets and croutons between them. Top with the pistachios and Parmesan.

CALORIES 379 —— FAT 15 G —— SAT FAT 4 G —— CARBS 41 G
SUGARS 2 G —— PROTEIN 22 G —— SODIUM 183 MG —— FIBER 5 G

POTATO SALAD
with Herring & Za'atar Yogurt

Pickled herrings, pearl onions, gherkins, and potatoes: the basis of a classic Dutch potato and herring salad. For some extra zing, I season the dressing with a generous pinch of za'atar, a spice blend widely used in Middle Eastern cuisine.

SERVES 2
PREPARATION TIME: 40 MINUTES

14 ounces (400 g) waxy potatoes, peeled
½ cup (60 g) thinly sliced peeled kohlrabi
Juice of ½ lime
4 pickled herring fillets, cut into ¾-inch (2 cm) pieces
4 gherkins, sliced
2 tablespoons pickled pearl onions, drained
2 tablespoons full-fat plain yogurt
1 tablespoon mayonnaise
2 teaspoons za'atar, plus extra
Salt, to taste
2 chervil sprigs, leaves only

Bring a large pot of salted water to a boil. Cook the potatoes until tender, 15 to 20 minutes. Drain and let cool. Cut the potatoes into bite-size pieces.

Meanwhile, mix the kohlrabi with the lime juice in a small bowl. Let sit for 5 minutes.

Mix the herring, gherkins, pearl onions, and kohlrabi with the potato in a large bowl.

In a small bowl, combine the yogurt, mayonnaise, and za'atar. Stir this dressing through the salad. Sprinkle with za'atar and salt and garnish with chervil.

CALORIES 318 —— FAT 14 G —— SAT FAT 3 G —— CARBS 35 G
SUGARS 25 G —— PROTEIN 15 G —— SODIUM 1,235 MG —— FIBER 6 G

THAI SALAD
with Spicy Calamari

I love the flavors of Thailand—the fresh veggies, spicy chiles, sweet and spicy ginger, sour lime, salty local fish sauce—and the smell of fresh cilantro. The strength of this punchy squid salad lies in the dressing and the crunchy vegetables.

SERVES 2
MARINATING TIME: 30 MINUTES
PREPARATION TIME: 25 MINUTES

DRESSING
½ garlic clove, finely minced
½ red bell pepper, seeded, finely
  chopped
1 tablespoon light olive oil
Juice of 1 lime
1½ tablespoons fish sauce
2 teaspoons sugar

1 garlic clove, coarsely chopped
¾-inch (2 cm) piece of ginger,
  peeled and coarsely chopped
1 teaspoon ground chile
Salt
2 tablespoons canola oil
6 medium squid, cleaned, tubes
  and tentacles separated
¼ head of napa cabbage, thinly
  sliced
1 red bell pepper, seeded, finely
  chopped
1 red onion, sliced into rings
½ medium cucumber, seeded and
  cut into long strips
2 scallions, sliced
1 tablespoon coarsely chopped
  peanuts
4 cilantro sprigs, leaves only

To make the dressing, whisk together the garlic, bell pepper, olive oil, lime juice, fish sauce, and sugar in a small bowl. Taste to see if the sweet-and-sour balance is right; add more lime juice or sugar, if necessary. Transfer to the refrigerator.

In a mortar, grind the garlic, ginger, chile, and a pinch of salt into a smooth paste. Blend in the canola oil. Transfer to a bowl and add the squid. Cover and marinate in the fridge for 30 minutes.

Meanwhile, toss the cabbage, bell pepper, onion, cucumber, and scallion together in a medium bowl. Cover and refrigerate.

Bring the squid to room temperature, about 5 minutes. Drain off the marinade.

Heat a large frying pan over high heat. Cook the squid tubes for 60 to 90 seconds, then flip them and add the tentacles to the pan. Cook for about 1 minute more.

Remove the squid from the pan and slice the tubes into ½-inch (13 mm) rings. Let cool to lukewarm.

Toss the squid and dressing with the vegetables. Divide the salad between two plates. Scatter the peanuts on top and garnish with cilantro.

CALORIES 670 —— FAT 31 G —— SAT FAT 4 G —— CARBS 40 G
SUGARS 16 G —— PROTEIN 60 G —— SODIUM 1,222 MG —— FIBER 7G

POTATO SALAD
with Turnip Greens & Hot-Smoked Salmon

Smoking not only helps to preserve fish, but also imparts a unique flavor that works really well in salads. Pressed for time? This potato salad with turnip greens is quick and easy to prepare.

SERVES 2
PREPARATION TIME: 30 MINUTES

10 to 11 ounces (300 g) baby waxy potatoes
Zest and juice of ½ lemon
3 tablespoons extra virgin olive oil
1 tablespoon red wine vinegar
Salt and pepper, to taste
2 cups (70 g) turnip greens or other leafy green vegetable
1 scallion, sliced
4 dill sprigs, leaves only, coarsely chopped
1 tablespoon capers, rinsed and drained
1 tablespoon chopped chives
5 ounces (150 g) skinless hot-smoked salmon, cut into chunks (see Tip)

> **TIP**: Take the salmon out of the fridge about 30 minutes before serving.

Bring a large pot of salted water to a boil. Cook the potatoes until tender, 15 to 20 minutes. Drain and cut in half. Transfer to a large bowl and let cool to lukewarm.

Add the lemon zest and juice, oil, and vinegar to the potatoes. Season with salt and pepper.

Toss the turnip greens, scallion, dill, capers, and chives with the potatoes. Carefully fold in the smoked salmon.

Serve the salad on plates or in shallow bowls.

CALORIES 398 — FAT 32 G — SAT FAT 5 G — CARBS 12 G
SUGARS 3 G — PROTEIN 20 G — SODIUM 612 MG — FIBER 5 G

PEAR & FIG SALAD
with Cod Liver & Orange Dressing

I love the taste of foie gras. But ever since I learned about the terrible conditions under which the ducks and geese are force-fed to make it, I no longer eat it. Cod liver is a tasty alternative, as it provides a similarly rich and fatty flavor. And by eating it, we're doing the ducks and geese a huge favor.

SERVES 2
PREPARATION TIME: 25 MINUTES

DRESSING
Zest of ½ orange
Juice of 2 oranges
Juice of 1 lime
1½ tablespoons sesame oil
2 teaspoons pink peppercorns,
   bruised
Salt, to taste

1 pear, cored and thinly sliced
3 fresh figs, stems removed,
   quartered
10 red grapes, halved
1 packed cup (50 g) beet greens or
   mixed greens, leaves only
One 4.3-ounce (120 g) can of cod
   liver, drained and coarsely
   chopped
2 tablespoons coarsely chopped
   walnuts
Flaky salt (like Maldon or fleur
   de sel)

To make the dressing, bring the orange juice to a boil in a small saucepan. Reduce the heat and simmer until the liquid has reduced by half, 5 to 8 minutes. Remove from the heat, transfer to a small bowl, and let cool.

Mix the cooled orange juice with the orange zest, lime juice, and sesame oil. Stir in the pink peppercorns and a pinch of salt. Cover and store in the fridge until you're ready to serve.

Divide the pear, figs, grapes, and beet greens between two plates. Top with pieces of cod liver. Drizzle on the dressing and sprinkle with the walnuts and flaky salt.

CALORIES 554 —— FAT 38 G —— SAT FAT 7 G —— CARBS 51 G
SUGARS 38 G —— PROTEIN 7 G —— SODIUM 280 MG —— FIBER 7 G

BRUNCH

NAVY BEAN SALAD
WITH CELERY, CARROT &
OCTOPUS — 87

SPINACH PANCAKES
WITH CREAM CHEESE, AVOCADO &
SMOKED SALMON — 88

BRUSCHETTA
WITH GRILLED VEGETABLES & COD
LIVER BUTTER — 91

GRILLED ZUCCHINI RIBBONS
WITH SMOKED SPRATS — 92

OLIVE & ANCHOVY FOCACCIA — 95

CHUNKY CRIOLLA
WITH MUSSELS — 98

KALE SALAD
WITH HAZELNUT, COCONUT &
TUNA — 101

STUFFED ZUCCHINI BLOSSOMS
WITH SAFFRON & ORANGE
DRESSING — 102

SPINACH & SALMON
SHAKSHUKA — 105

BAKED POTATOES
WITH VEGETABLES &
CRAYFISH — 106

Officially, brunch is a combination of breakfast and lunch, usually eaten in the late morning. But please don't take this too literally. In this chapter, I've brought together a selection of small dishes that can be enjoyed at any time of the day, and even on festive occasions. They're particularly good for sharing.

NAVY BEAN SALAD
with Celery, Carrot & Octopus

Octopus has a lovely meaty texture. The trick is to simmer it very slowly over low heat. In this recipe, I cook the octopus in water and then let it sit in the liquid, off the heat, for at least another half hour to allow it to tenderize further. Using fish broth would work perfectly, too.

SERVES 2
COOKING TIME: 1 HOUR AND
30 MINUTES
PREPARATION TIME: 25 MINUTES

1 octopus (about 2 pounds/1 kg), thawed if frozen
10 black peppercorns
1 bay leaf
7 ounces (200 g) waxy potatoes, peeled
½ cup (100 g) canned navy beans, rinsed and drained
½ celery stalk, thinly sliced
1 small carrot, peeled and thinly sliced
6 cherry tomatoes, quartered
10 kalamata olives, pitted
½ red chile, sliced into thin rings
4 thyme sprigs, leaves only
2 flat-leaf parsley sprigs, leaves only
2 tablespoons extra virgin olive oil
Salt and pepper, to taste

Place a large pot of salted cold water on the stovetop and add the octopus, peppercorns, and bay leaf. Bring to a boil, then reduce the heat and cover. Let the octopus simmer gently for 30 minutes. Turn off the heat and let sit for another 30 minutes, until soft and cooked through.

Drain the octopus and separate the tentacles. You'll need about 7 ounces (200 g) of tentacles; any leftover tentacles can be frozen.

Meanwhile, bring a large pot of salted water to a boil over medium-high heat. Cook the potatoes until tender, 15 to 20 minutes. Drain and let cool before cutting into chunks.

Carefully combine the octopus, potatoes, beans, celery, carrot, tomatoes, olives, chile, thyme, and parsley in a large bowl and dress with the olive oil. Season with salt and pepper.

Divide the salad between two plates or serve from the bowl.

CALORIES 385 —— FAT 20 G —— SAT FAT 2 G —— CARBS 32 G
SUGARS 6 G —— PROTEIN 23 G —— SODIUM 595 MG —— FIBER 8 G

SPINACH PANCAKES
with Cream Cheese, Avocado & Smoked Salmon

Getting children to eat their greens can be a challenge—I speak from experience. These spinach pancakes, which I make with my two youngest children, Juul and Ties, are always a big hit. In fact, they're great for hiding all kinds of leafy vegetables.

SERVES 2
PREPARATION TIME: 30 MINUTES

Generous 3 cups (100 g) spinach
1 cup (240 ml) milk
3 eggs
1 cup (120 g) all-purpose flour
Salt and pepper, to taste
1 red onion, sliced into rings
Juice of 1 lime
1½ tablespoons butter
Scant ½ cup (7 tablespoons/100 g) cream cheese
1 avocado, pitted, peeled, and diced
About 5 ounces (150 g) cold-smoked wild sockeye salmon
6 cherry tomatoes, quartered
Handful of arugula leaves
3 dill sprigs, leaves only, coarsely chopped
Extra virgin olive oil

Purée the spinach and milk with an immersion blender or in a food processor. Mix in 1 of the eggs, followed by the flour. Season with a pinch of salt. Set the batter aside.

Combine the red onion and lime juice in a small bowl. Let stand for 10 minutes before draining off the liquid. Set aside.

Meanwhile, bring enough water to cover the remaining 2 eggs to a boil in a small pot. Add the eggs and cook for about 8 minutes, until hard-boiled. Cool them under cold running water, then peel. Press them through a sieve using the back of a spoon. Set aside.

Melt half of the butter in a medium frying pan over medium-high heat and swirl to evenly coat the pan. Pour half of the batter into the pan and cook until the bottom is golden brown, 2 to 3 minutes. Put a lid on after about 1 minute so the top sets. Transfer the pancake to a plate and keep warm. Repeat with the remaining butter and batter.

Spread the pancakes with cream cheese and scatter on the avocado. Top with the smoked salmon and tomato, followed by the marinated onion, arugula, and dill. Drizzle with olive oil and finish with a sprinkling of egg and freshly ground pepper.

CALORIES 966 — FAT 59 G — SAT FAT 25 G — CARBS 69 G
SUGARS 14 G — PROTEIN 44 G — SODIUM 1,405 MG — FIBER 9 G

BRUSCHETTA
with Grilled Vegetables & Cod Liver Butter

I'm a big proponent of eating (almost) the entire fish. That's to say, not just the familiar parts, like fillet. Why not try the cheeks or, as in this dish, the liver? This is bruschetta my way, with zucchini, eggplant, bell pepper, and cod liver butter.

SERVES 2
PREPARATION TIME: 40 MINUTES

COD LIVER BUTTER
2 ounces (50 g) drained canned
    cod liver
3 tablespoons butter, diced and
    softened
2 teaspoons brandy
Salt and white pepper, to taste

½ medium zucchini, cut into
    ¼-inch-thick (6 mm) slices
½ medium eggplant, cut into
    ¼-inch-thick (6 mm) slices
1 bell pepper, seeded and sliced
Pepper, to taste
3 thyme sprigs, leaves only
Extra virgin olive oil
1 baguette, halved horizontally
Balsamic vinegar
2 basil sprigs, leaves only

TIP: If the vegetables are still warm enough after you place them on the bread, you can let the cod liver butter melt onto them outside the oven.

To make the butter, press the cod liver through a fine sieve into a small bowl, using the back of a spoon. Mix in the butter and brandy to form a smooth paste. Season with salt and white pepper. Spoon the mixture onto a piece of plastic wrap and roll into a log. Let it set in the fridge for a minimum of 30 minutes.

While the butter is chilling, preheat the oven to 350°F (180°C).

Line a baking sheet with parchment paper. Arrange the zucchini, eggplant, and bell pepper on it. Sprinkle with salt, black pepper, and thyme, and drizzle with olive oil. Roast the vegetables for about 20 minutes, until they're beginning to char.

While the vegetables are roasting, place the baguette halves on a rack in the oven and bake for 5 to 7 minutes, until crisp and golden brown. Remove from the oven.

Remove the vegetables from the oven. Transfer them to a bowl, stir in a few drops of olive oil, and season with salt and black pepper.

Top the bread with the vegetables and drizzle with vinegar. Dot the cod liver butter on the vegetables and return the bruschetta to the oven for another 2 minutes, until the cod liver starts to melt. Garnish with the basil and an extra trickle of vinegar.

CALORIES 809 —— FAT 38 G —— SAT FAT 14 G —— CARBS 98 G
SUGARS 6 G —— PROTEIN 19 G —— SODIUM 1,064 MG —— FIBER 7 G

GRILLED ZUCCHINI RIBBONS
with Smoked Sprats

These zucchini ribbons are briefly grilled and seasoned with vinegar and oil before being topped with smoked sprats. The small oily fish add a pleasant smoky note to this quick and tasty dish.

SERVES 2
PREPARATION TIME: 20 MINUTES

2 medium zucchini (green or yellow, or 1 of each)
4 tablespoons (60 ml) extra virgin olive oil
Salt and pepper, to taste
1 tablespoon raw, unsalted sunflower seeds
1 tablespoon raw, unsalted pumpkin seeds
2 teaspoons red wine vinegar
4 ounces (120 g) smoked sprats, filleted (see page 243)

Slice the zucchini into long, thin ribbons using a mandoline. In a medium bowl, combine the ribbons with 2 tablespoons of the olive oil. Season with salt.

Toast the sunflower and pumpkin seeds in a dry pan over medium-high heat until golden brown, about 3 minutes. Remove from the pan and set aside.

Heat a grill pan over medium-high heat and grill the zucchini ribbons until grill marks develop, 1 to 2 minutes on each side. Transfer the zucchini to a bowl, add the remaining 2 tablespoons olive oil and the vinegar, and mix. Season with salt and pepper.

Arrange the zucchini on a platter and scatter the toasted seeds on top. Serve with the smoked sprats on the side.

CALORIES 481 —— FAT 44 G —— SAT FAT 8 G —— CARBS 8 G
SUGAR 4 G —— PROTEIN 16 G —— SODIUM 234 MG —— FIBER 3 G

OLIVE & ANCHOVY FOCACCIA

Focaccia is the perfect brunch dish. I like to top it with anchovies, capers, and cherry tomatoes. But whatever the topping, everybody loves focaccia. Why not make some with lots of veggies!

SERVES 4
RISING TIME: 1 HOUR AND
20 MINUTES
PREPARATION TIME: 20 MINUTES

4 cups (500 g) all-purpose flour,
    plus extra for kneading
½ teaspoon salt
One ¼-ounce (7 g) packet of
    instant dry yeast
⅓ cup (80 ml) light olive oil
3 tablespoons pitted, sliced
    kalamata olives
2 tablespoons capers, rinsed and
    drained
One 1.6-ounce (43 g) can of
    anchovies packed in oil, drained
10 to 12 cherry tomatoes, halved
1 tablespoon dried oregano
Flaky salt (like Maldon or fleur de
    sel), to taste

Combine the flour, salt, and yeast in a large bowl. Stir in 2 tablespoons of the olive oil until you have a crumbly texture. Add 1¼ cups (300 ml) lukewarm water and stir. Sprinkle some flour on a work surface. Turn the dough out of the bowl and knead until smooth, 3 to 5 minutes.

Place the dough in a clean bowl and cover with plastic wrap or a damp kitchen towel. Let it rest for 1 hour at room temperature, to allow the dough to rise slightly.

Line a baking sheet with parchment paper. Turn out the dough onto the baking sheet and use your hands to spread it into a flat, even layer about ¾-inch (2 cm) thick, then dimple the dough with your fingers. Let rise for another 20 minutes.

Meanwhile, preheat the oven to 425°F (220°C).

Gently press the olives, capers, and anchovies into the dough. Do the same with the tomatoes, then scatter the oregano on top. Drizzle with the remaining olive oil and sprinkle with salt.

Bake the focaccia for 10 to 12 minutes, until golden brown. Let cool and then serve.

CALORIES 654 —— FAT 22 G —— SAT FAT 3 G —— CARBS 97 G
SUGARS 2 G —— PROTEIN 163 G —— SODIUM 837 MG —— FIBER 4 G

CHUNKY CRIOLLA
with Mussels

Criolla is a Latin American garnish made of finely diced red onion, tomato, and chile. In this recipe, the vegetables are chopped quite coarsely to produce something closer to a salad. Sweet-briny mussels are great with the tangy vegetables.

SERVES 2
PREPARATION TIME: 25 MINUTES

Generous 1 pound (500 g) mussels in the shell
1 tablespoon vegetable oil, for frying
1 garlic clove, thinly sliced
1 celery stalk, sliced
Salt and pepper, to taste
1 red onion, sliced into rings
1 tablespoon extra virgin olive oil, plus extra for drizzling (optional)
Zest and juice of 1 lime
4 cilantro sprigs, leaves only, chopped, plus extra for serving
3 medium tomatoes, seeded and cut into ¾-inch (2 cm) chunks
1 ají amarillo or red chile, seeded and thinly sliced
2 tablespoons corn kernels (home-cooked, thawed frozen, or drained canned)

Wash the mussels under cold running water and discard any with broken or open shells. Drain.

Heat the oil in a large, deep frying pan over medium-high heat. Braise the garlic and celery, stirring occasionally, until softened, 2 to 3 minutes. Season with salt and pepper.

Add the mussels, turn up the heat, and cover. Give the pan a shake every now and then and cook for 3 to 5 minutes. The mussels are done when they've opened. Remove from the pan and let cool. Discard the garlic-celery mixture.

Remove the mussel meats from the shells and set aside. Discard the shells.

Meanwhile, soak the onion rings in ice water for 10 minutes. Drain, then pat dry with a paper towel.

Toss the onion with the olive oil, lime juice, and cilantro in a large bowl. Add the tomatoes, chile, and corn. Fold in the mussels and season with salt and pepper. Sprinkle with lime zest and drizzle on some extra olive oil (if you like). Garnish with extra cilantro.

CALORIES 417 —— FAT 20 G —— SAT FAT 3 G —— CARBS 28 G
SUGAR 11 G —— PROTEIN 33 G —— SODIUM 754 MG —— FIBER 4 G

KALE SALAD
with Hazelnut, Coconut & Tuna

Fishermen in the Maldives use the sustainable pole-and-line method to catch the most delicious tuna. I regularly visit Laamu Atoll, where I eat this simple but incredibly tasty dish: pita bread filled with a mixture of tuna, coconut, hazelnuts, and locally grown cabbage. For this recipe, I've replaced the cabbage with kale.

SERVES 2
PREPARATION TIME: 15 MINUTES

3 cups (100 g) finely chopped kale, leaves only
1 small yellow onion, finely chopped
2 jalapeños, seeded and very finely chopped
Zest and juice of 1 lime
½ teaspoon salt
1 cup (100 g) freshly grated coconut, or ⅔ cup (60 g) desiccated coconut mixed with 1 tablespoon coconut milk
One 5-ounce (142 g) can of tuna in water, drained
1 tablespoon coarsely chopped roasted and blanched hazelnuts
2 pieces of pita bread

Using your hands, massage the kale with the onion, jalapeño, lime juice, and salt in a large bowl until the leaves start to soften and wilt, 2 to 3 minutes. Stir in the coconut and tuna. Scatter the hazelnuts and lime zest on top and serve with the pita.

CALORIES 462 —— FAT 22 G —— SAT FAT 15 G —— CARBS 51 G
SUGAR 10 G —— PROTEIN 26 G —— SODIUM 1,173 MG —— FIBER 8 G

STUFFED ZUCCHINI BLOSSOMS
with Saffron & Orange Dressing

We eat a lot of zucchini in the US, but we're much less familiar with their flowers. And that's a shame, because zucchini flowers are full of flavor, and very pretty, too. In this oven dish, they're stuffed with crayfish and cauliflower—but feel free to experiment with other ingredients. Any leftover dressing will keep, covered, in the fridge for several days.

SERVES 2
PREPARATION TIME: 40 MINUTES

SAFFRON & ORANGE DRESSING
2 tablespoons sherry vinegar
1 tablespoon white wine
10 to 12 saffron threads
½ teaspoon brown sugar
Zest of ¼ orange
Juice of ½ orange
Juice of ½ lemon
Scant ½ cup (100 ml) extra virgin
   olive oil
Salt and pepper, to taste

2 cups (200 g) cauliflower florets
5 ounces (150 g) crayfish, cooked
   and peeled
⅓ cup (70 g) ricotta
¼ teaspoon grated nutmeg
½ teaspoon smoked paprika
1 tablespoon extra virgin olive oil,
   plus extra for greasing the pan
White pepper, to taste
6 zucchini blossoms
1½ teaspoons bread crumbs
1 tablespoon coarsely chopped
   roasted and blanched hazelnuts

Preheat the oven to 375°F (190°C).

To make the dressing, mix the sherry vinegar with the wine in a small saucepan. Add the saffron. Steep the saffron for 10 minutes, until the liquid is brightly colored. Add the sugar and orange zest and heat over medium-high heat. Stir until the sugar dissolves, 1 to 2 minutes. Pour the liquid into a bowl.

Pour the orange juice into the saucepan. Place over low heat and reduce by half. Add to the saffron mixture and let cool.

Whisk in the lemon juice and olive oil. Season with salt and pepper.

Bring a medium pot of salted water to a boil. Cook the cauliflower florets until tender, about 5 minutes. Drain and let cool.

Mince the crayfish and cauliflower and transfer to a large bowl. Mix in the ricotta, nutmeg, paprika, and olive oil. Season with salt and white pepper.

Trim the stems of the zucchini blossoms. Carefully open the blossoms by folding back the petals. Remove the stamens and pistils and fill with the crayfish-cauliflower mixture. Close the blossoms by folding the petals inward and pinching them shut with your fingers.

Grease a baking dish with olive oil and arrange the zucchini blossoms in it. Sprinkle with the bread crumbs and hazelnuts. Bake for 6 to 8 minutes, until lightly colored and heated through.

Serve with the dressing.

CALORIES 482 — FAT 41 G — SAT FAT 9 G — CARBS 14 G
SUGARS 8 G — PROTEIN 18 G — SODIUM 152 MG — FIBER 3 G

SPINACH & SALMON SHAKSHUKA

Who doesn't love this famous dish from the Middle East? I make this shakshuka not with the typical tomatoes but instead with a creamy combination of spinach and salmon. The harissa adds a nice kick to the sauce. Here I use the green variety, which is a bit spicier than the red one.

SERVES 2
PREPARATION TIME: 25 MINUTES

½ teaspoon cumin seeds
½ teaspoon fennel seeds
½ teaspoon grated nutmeg
2 tablespoons light olive oil
1 to 2 teaspoons green harissa (or red, if you prefer)
10 cups (400 g) chopped mature spinach
1 garlic clove, peeled
2 eggs
½ cup (120 ml) light cream
4 ounces (120 g) salmon fillet, skin removed, cut into chunks
3 dill sprigs, leaves only, finely chopped, plus extra
Salt and pepper, to taste
⅓ cup (40 g) soft goat cheese

Grind the cumin and fennel seeds in a mortar. Mix in the nutmeg.

Heat the oil in a large frying pan over medium-high heat and sauté the harissa, cumin, fennel, and nutmeg until warmed, 1 minute. Add the spinach. Stick the garlic clove on a fork and use it to continuously stir the spinach and infuse it with a mild garlic aroma. Lower the heat once the spinach has completely wilted, 3 to 4 minutes. Add 1 tablespoon of water if the mixture becomes too dry. Discard the garlic.

Separate the eggs, whites in one small bowl, yolks in another, being careful to keep the yolks intact. Mix the cream into the egg whites, then add to the spinach mixture and blend thoroughly. Add the salmon and stir to combine. Reduce the cream mixture by half over low heat, 5 to 7 minutes. Sprinkle on the dill and season with salt and pepper. Crumble the goat cheese on top.

Make two wells in the mixture and slide an egg yolk into each. Put the lid on and cook until the yolks set, 5 to 7 minutes.

Serve immediately, topped with extra dill.

CALORIES   518 ——— FAT   42   G ——— SAT   FAT   13   G ——— CARBS   11   G
SUGARS   2   G ——— PROTEIN   28   G ——— SODIUM   385   MG ——— FIBER   6   G

BAKED POTATOES
with Vegetables & Crayfish

I love sea vegetables. Sea fennel, or rock samphire, is a new variety that's available online or in specialty stores. It's a great alternative to the better-known marsh samphire and sea lavender. The sea fennel garnish adds a nice briny, anise note to these traditional baked potatoes with crème fraîche.

SERVES 2
POTATO BAKING TIME: 1 HOUR
PREPARATION TIME: 15 MINUTES

4 medium baking (russet)
   potatoes
Extra virgin olive oil
Salt and pepper, to taste
8 green asparagus tips
2 tablespoons crème fraîche
1 tablespoon full-fat plain yogurt
Zest and juice of ¼ lemon
1 teaspoon grated horseradish
3 dill sprigs, leaves only, finely
   chopped
3 cups (100 g) watercress, leaves
   only
4 ounces (120 g) crayfish tails,
   cooked and peeled
1 scallion, sliced
4 sea fennel sprigs, or marsh
   samphire or sea aster
2 tablespoons salmon roe

Preheat the oven to 425°F (220°C).

Pierce the potatoes and place on a sheet of aluminum foil. Drizzle with olive oil, season with salt, and wrap the foil around them, leaving a small opening at the top. Bake for 40 to 60 minutes, until soft and cooked through.

Meanwhile, bring a medium saucepan of generously salted water to a boil. Blanch the asparagus for 2 to 3 minutes, until bright green. Drain, then run under cold water to stop the cooking process. Pat dry with a kitchen towel. Set aside.

Make the sauce by combining the crème fraîche and yogurt in a small bowl. Stir in the lemon juice, horseradish, and dill. Season with salt and pepper. Store in the fridge until ready to use.

Take the potatoes out of the oven and remove the foil. Make a slit in the top of each potato with a spoon and scoop out some of the flesh to create a bowl (save the flesh for another recipe). Fill with a dollop of the creamy sauce, scatter on the watercress, and top with the crayfish, scallion, and asparagus. Grind on some pepper and garnish with the sea fennel, salmon roe, and lemon zest. Serve any remaining sauce separately.

CALORIES 235 —— FAT 14 G —— SAT FAT 5 G —— CARBS 14 G
SUGARS 3 G —— PROTEIN 15 G —— SODIUM 151 MG —— FIBER 7 G

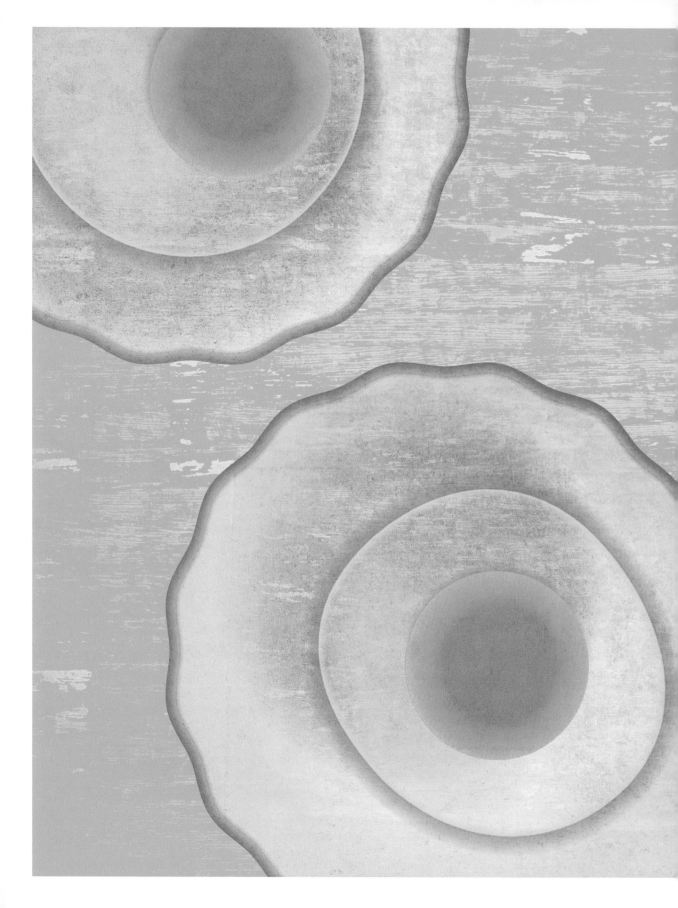

SNACKS & SANDWICHES

Whether you enjoy them with drinks, as a substantial and nutritious lunch, after a night out, or as a quick snack, the recipes in this chapter should provide plenty of inspiration for you to get creative in the kitchen and to experiment with different ingredients. And remember, it's always best to use seasonable vegetables that look fresh and are full of flavor.

VEGETABLE CHIPS
with Fried Shrimp & Aïoli

Here's the perfect appetizer platter to enjoy with drinks: deep-fried, wafer-thin chips made of colorful vegetables, plus shrimp. The small, unpeeled shrimp are fried whole alongside the veggies. Homemade aïoli is great with both.

SERVES 2
PREPARATION TIME: 1 HOUR

1 medium cassava (yuca), peeled
1 medium sweet potato, peeled
2 medium beets, peeled
1 medium carrot, peeled
Oil, for frying
4 Tuscan kale leaves
Salt, to taste
5 ounces (150 g) unpeeled small shrimp
Flaky salt (like Maldon or fleur de sel), for serving
1 recipe Aïoli (page 237), for serving

Thinly slice the cassava, sweet potato, beets, and carrot using a mandoline or vegetable peeler. Let them dry on a rack, without overlapping, for 30 minutes.

Fill a medium saucepan with 2 inches (5 cm) of oil and heat the oil to 325°F (170°C). Fry the sliced vegetables and kale, in batches, until crunchy, up to 2 minutes per batch. Remove with a skimmer, drain slightly on a paper towel, and season with salt. Fry the shrimp in the same oil for about 1 minute, until crisp. Drain well on a paper towel.

Serve with flaky salt and aïoli on the side.

CALORIES 833 —— FAT 46 G —— SAT FAT 6 G —— CARBS 90 G
SUGARS 11 G —— PROTEIN 22 G —— SODIUM 242 MG —— FIBER 9 G

TOMATO SALAD
with Squid and Pol Sambol

Sri Lanka's national condiment is called pol sambol. It's not to be confused with the more familiar sambal oelek, which contains lots of fiery red chile. Pol sambol is milder and made with grated coconut.

SERVES 2
PREPARATION TIME: 40 MINUTES

FLATBREAD
1⅓ cups (170 g) all-purpose flour
½ teaspoon baking powder
¼ teaspoon salt
⅔ cup (170 g) full-fat plain yogurt

POL SAMBOL
1 small red onion, minced
1 red chile, seeded and minced
1 garlic clove, minced
Juice of ½ lime
Salt, to taste
1 medium tomato, seeded and
  finely chopped
1 cup (100 g) grated fresh coconut
  (see Tip)
2 cilantro sprigs, leaves only, finely
  chopped

TOMATO SALAD
7 ounces (200 g) mixed tomatoes,
  coarsely chopped
½ red onion, sliced into rings
2 cilantro sprigs, leaves only,
  coarsely chopped
2 tablespoons extra virgin olive oil
2 teaspoons white wine vinegar
Pepper, to taste

LIME YOGURT
¼ cup (65 g) full-fat plain yogurt
Zest and juice of 1 lime

SQUID RINGS
¾ cup (100 g) all-purpose flour
1 teaspoon smoked paprika
About 7 ounces (200 g) squid tubes,
  cleaned and sliced into rings
Oil, for frying

To make the flatbread, mix the flour with the baking powder, salt, and yogurt in a large bowl and knead into a smooth dough. Divide into four balls and set aside, covered with a damp kitchen towel.

To make the pol sambol, combine the onion, chile, garlic, lime juice, and ½ teaspoon of salt in a medium bowl and mix with your hands (wear disposable gloves to protect your hands from the chile). Add the tomato, coconut, and cilantro and mix. Set aside.

Roll out the dough balls into four thin flatbreads. Cook, one at a time, in a dry frying pan over medium-high heat until nicely browned, 3 to 4 minutes on each side. Transfer to a plate and keep warm, covered with a clean towel.

To make the salad, mix the tomatoes with the onion and cilantro in a medium bowl. Season with olive oil, vinegar, salt, and pepper. Set aside.

To make the lime yogurt, mix the ingredients in a small bowl. Set aside.

To make the squid, spread the flour on a plate and mix in the paprika. Dredge the pieces of squid in the mixture.

Fill a deep saucepan with about 1¼ inches (3 cm) of oil and heat to 350°F (180°C). Fry the squid, in batches, until golden brown, 40 to 60 seconds. Remove with a skimmer and drain on a paper towel. Sprinkle with salt.

Serve the flatbreads with the tomato salad, pol sambol, squid, and yogurt.

> **TIP**: If you can't find a fresh coconut, use an equal amount of desiccated coconut plus 1 to 2 teaspoons of coconut cream.

CALORIES 1,117 —— FAT 52 G —— SAT FAT 22 G —— CARBS 129 G
SUGAR 24 G —— PROTEIN 37 G —— SODIUM 545 MG —— FIBER 12 G

EGGS SUNNY-SIDE UP
with Peas, Sea Purslane & Anchovies

Peas with pork belly—it doesn't get more traditionally Dutch than that. In this take on a classic, I've replaced the pork with goat cheese and anchovies. Anchovies are fantastic to use as an umami kick in so many dishes. Here, I melt them to give this dish an extra level of flavor.

SERVES 2
PREPARATION TIME: 20 MINUTES

½ cup (70 g) peas (shelled fresh or frozen)
Extra virgin olive oil
1 garlic clove, minced
4 salted anchovy fillets, soaked to remove excess salt and drained
½ medium tomato, seeded and diced (I used a yellow tomato)
1½ cups (60 g) sea purslane
2 scallions, sliced
2 eggs
⅓ cup (40 g) soft goat cheese
4 slices of rustic or sourdough bread
2 flat-leaf parsley sprigs, leaves only
2 chervil sprigs, leaves only
Flaky salt (like Maldon or fleur de sel)
Pepper

Bring a medium saucepan of water to a boil. Cook the peas until fork-tender, 6 to 9 minutes. Drain, then run under cold water to stop the cooking process. Pat dry with a kitchen towel.

Place a large frying pan over medium heat. When the pan is hot, pour in 2 tablespoons of olive oil and sauté the garlic and anchovies for 1 minute, making sure not to let the garlic brown. Add the peas, tomato, sea purslane, and scallions and sauté, stirring constantly, for 2 minutes.

Lower the heat and create a well in the vegetable mixture. Crack the eggs into it, crumble the goat cheese onto the vegetables, and cover with a lid. Cook until the eggs are just set, about 4 minutes.

Meanwhile, toast the bread.

Sprinkle the dish with the parsley, chervil, flaky salt, and pepper. Serve with the toast.

CALORIES 487 —— FAT 26 G —— SAT FAT 7 G —— CARBS 42 G
SUGARS 4 G —— PROTEIN 21 G —— SODIUM 1,129 MG —— FIBER 5 G

LATKES
with Smoked Mackerel, Apple & Parsley

Latkes are a staple of Jewish cooking. These crispy fritters, made from grated potato and onion, are similar to Swiss rösti. The apple and capers are an excellent foil for the fried potato and the oily smoked mackerel.

SERVES 2
PREPARATION TIME: 45 MINUTES

- 8 to 9 ounces (250 g) starchy potatoes, peeled and coarsely grated
- 1 medium onion, coarsely grated
- 2 eggs
- 2 teaspoons all-purpose flour or matzo meal
- Salt and pepper, to taste
- Light olive oil, for frying
- 3 to 4 ounces (100 g) smoked mackerel fillets, skin removed, torn into pieces
- 1 tablespoon crème fraîche
- 1 tablespoon mayonnaise
- 1 teaspoon Dijon mustard
- Zest and juice of ½ lemon
- 4 flat-leaf parsley sprigs, leaves only, finely chopped
- 1 teaspoon capers, rinsed and drained, plus extra for serving
- ½ Granny Smith apple, cored and julienned, plus extra for serving

Preheat the oven to 350°F (180°C).

Place the potato and onion in a piece of cheesecloth or a clean kitchen towel and tie the ends together. Place in a sieve and let the potato and onion drain for 20 minutes.

Meanwhile, bring enough water to cover an egg to a boil in a small pot. Add 1 of the eggs and cook for about 8 minutes, until hard-boiled. Cool under cold running water, then peel. Press the egg through a sieve using the back of a spoon. Set aside.

Squeeze out any excess liquid from the potatoes and onion, and transfer them to a large bowl. Beat the remaining egg in a small bowl. Add it to the potato-onion mixture along with the flour. Season with salt and pepper. Shape the mixture into little round cakes, 2 inches (5 cm) in diameter.

Heat 2 tablespoons oil in a large frying pan over medium-high heat. Fry the latkes, in batches if necessary, until golden brown on the bottom, about 1 minute. Flip them with a slotted spatula, being careful not to let them fall apart, then fry for another minute. Add more oil to the pan if needed. Transfer them to a rack set over a baking sheet. Bake for 8 to 10 minutes, until crispy on the outside and cooked through on the inside.

Meanwhile, mash the mackerel fillet in a small bowl with a fork. Stir in the crème fraîche, mayonnaise, mustard, and lemon zest and juice. Fold in the parsley and capers. Season with pepper.

Top the latkes with the mackerel mixture and garnish with more capers, the apple, and the sieved egg. Finish with freshly ground pepper.

CALORIES 458 —— FAT 33 G —— SAT FAT 8 G —— CARBS 19 G
SUGARS 9 G —— PROTEIN 23 G —— SODIUM 425 MG —— FIBER 5 G

PAN BAGNAT

Pan bagnat translates literally to "wet bread." It's a classic from the South of France—think salade niçoise, but on bread. This generously filled bread is tightly wrapped in plastic and then left to sit in the fridge for several hours to allow the flavors and juices to meld. Perfect for a road trip or a sunny picnic.

SERVES 4 TO 6
PREPARATION TIME: 30 MINUTES
REFRIGERATION TIME: 4 TO
6 HOURS

2 to 3 ounces (50 g) haricots verts, trimmed
½ cup (50 g) shelled, peeled fresh fava beans
2 eggs
1 round loaf of crusty bread, sliced horizontally one-third of the way from the top
4 tablespoons extra virgin olive oil
2 tablespoons white wine vinegar
2 medium tomatoes, sliced
4 cooked artichoke hearts (from a can or jar), coarsely chopped
2 radishes, thinly sliced
1 scallion, sliced
One 5-ounce (142 g) can of tuna in oil, drained
4 salted anchovy fillets, soaked to remove excess salt and drained
3 basil sprigs, leaves only
Salt and pepper, to taste

Fill a bowl with ice water. Bring a medium saucepan of generously salted water to a boil. Cook the green beans for 5 to 7 minutes, adding the fava beans after about 4 minutes, until all of the vegetables are tender-crisp. Scoop them out of the pan with a skimmer and transfer them immediately to the ice water to cool. Drain, then pat dry with a kitchen towel.

Meanwhile, bring enough water to cover the eggs to a boil in a small pot. Add the eggs and cook for about 8 minutes, until hard-boiled. Cool under cold running water. Peel, then thinly slice.

Hollow out the bottom part of the loaf. (Save the insides for another use, such as bread crumbs.) Drizzle the inside with 2 tablespoons of the olive oil and 1 tablespoon of the vinegar.

Layer the filling inside the bread: Begin with the tomato, followed by the artichoke, radish, scallion, eggs, and the green beans and fava beans. Top with the tuna, anchovies, and basil. Season with salt and pepper and drizzle with the remaining 2 tablespoons olive oil and 1 tablespoon vinegar.

Cover with the top of the loaf and tightly wrap the loaf with two layers of plastic wrap. Let it sit in the fridge for 4 to 6 hours to blend all the different flavors.

Cut the sandwich into wedges to serve.

CALORIES 496 —— FAT 17 G —— SAT FAT 3 G —— CARBS 66 G
SUGARS 7 G —— PROTEIN 20 G —— SODIUM 905 MG —— FIBER 5 G

SEA LAVENDER & WATER SPINACH
with Shrimp & Tarragon Cream

In my version of shrimp on toast, I use extra vegetables, like water spinach and sea lavender. Water spinach grows in damp soil and can be eaten raw or cooked, just like normal spinach. I like to serve it with a creamy tarragon sauce instead of the typical mayonnaise.

SERVES 2
PREPARATION TIME: 20 MINUTES

TARRAGON CREAM
4 tarragon sprigs, leaves only,
　finely chopped
Salt, to taste
2 teaspoons Dijon mustard
1 tablespoon white wine vinegar
3 tablespoons light cream

Oil, for frying
1 cup (40 g) sea lavender or marsh
　samphire
1 cup (40 g) water spinach
4 slices of sourdough bread
1½ cups (150 g) cooked small
　shrimp, peeled
¼ mango, diced, at room
　temperature
1 tablespoon black tobiko
Salt and pepper, to taste

To make the tarragon cream, grind the tarragon with a pinch of salt in a mortar. Transfer to a small bowl and stir in the mustard and vinegar until smooth. Stir in the cream and season with salt. Set aside.

Heat a splash of oil in a small frying pan over medium-high heat and sauté the sea lavender and water spinach for 1 to 2 minutes, until softened. Remove from the pan and let cool slightly.

Toast the bread.

Arrange the sea lavender and spinach on the slices of toast. Pour some of the tarragon cream over the vegetables, then top with the shrimp, mango, and tobiko. Season with salt and pepper.

Serve with the remaining tarragon cream on the side.

CALORIES 381 —— FAT 15 G —— SAT FAT 4 G —— CARBS 40 G
SUGARS 5 G —— PROTEIN 21 G —— SODIUM 903 MG —— FIBER 3 G

CRUDITÉS
with Anchoïade & Tapenade

Anchoïade is a classic anchovy sauce that can be served either warm or cold. It's great as a dip for raw vegetables, aka crudités, and is also lovely with roasted vegetables, on bread, and as a salad dressing.

SERVES 4 TO 6
PREPARATION TIME: 1 HOUR AND
30 MINUTES

ANCHOÏADE
1½ ounces (45 g) salted anchovy
   fillets
Scant ½ cup (100 ml) milk
1 tablespoon white wine vinegar
½ garlic clove
5 kalamata olives, pitted
2 tablespoons plus 1 teaspoon
   grapeseed oil
2 tablespoons plus 1 teaspoon light
   olive oil

TAPENADE
1½ cups (200 g) kalamata olives,
   pitted
1 garlic clove, halved
½ ounce (15 g) salted anchovy
   fillets
3 tablespoons capers, rinsed and
   drained
1 basil sprig, leaves only, finely
   chopped
1 tablespoon sherry vinegar
2 tablespoons extra virgin olive oil

1 lemon, halved
1 tablespoon all-purpose flour
1 teaspoon salt
1 artichoke
3 broccolini stalks
1 cup (100 g) cauliflower florets
   (any color you like)
1 medium cucumber, seeded and
   cut into strips
2 bell peppers, seeded and cut
   into strips

5 medium carrots, peeled and
   halved lengthwise
2 heads of Belgian endive, leaves
   separated
1 bunch of radishes, stems
   trimmed to ¼ inch (6 mm), leaves
   discarded

To make the anchoïade, soak the anchovy fillets in the milk for 30 minutes to remove excess salt. Drain and pat dry with a paper towel.

Blend the anchovies with 1½ tablespoons water, the vinegar, garlic, and olives in a blender or food processor until thoroughly combined. Add the grapeseed and light olive oils in a slow, steady trickle while continuing to blend. Transfer the anchoïade to a container, cover, and chill in the fridge for 30 minutes. Wash and dry the blender.

To make the tapenade, pulse the olives with the garlic, anchovy fillets, and capers until a grainy paste forms. Transfer to a container. Spoon in the basil, vinegar, and extra virgin olive oil, and stir to mix. Cover and chill in the fridge for 30 minutes.

While the anchoïade and tapenade are chilling, bring a medium pot of water to a boil over high heat. Add the lemon, flour, and salt. Remove the artichoke stem by wrenching it back and forth until it comes off. Cook the artichoke until tender, 35 to 45 minutes. It's done when the tip of a sharp knife slides into the bottom with ease. Drain the artichoke and let cool.

Bring a small saucepan of water to a boil. Blanch the broccolini and cauliflower until tender-crisp, 2 to 3 minutes. Drain and run under cold water to stop the cooking process. Pat dry with a kitchen towel.

Arrange the artichoke, broccolini, cauliflower, cucumber, bell pepper, carrots, endive, and radishes on a platter. Serve with the anchoïade and tapenade for dipping.

CALORIES 325 —— FAT 25 G —— SAT FAT 3 G —— CARBS 22 G
SUGARS 8 G —— PROTEIN 10 G —— SODIUM 908 MG —— FIBER 10 G

GREEN PEA GUACAMOLE ROLLS
with Pulled Salmon

Hot-smoked salmon—briefly cooked at around 150°F (65°C)—has a beautiful smoky flavor and tender texture. The salmon can be pulled apart quite easily, hence "pulled salmon." It really complements this green pea and avocado guacamole.

SERVES 2
PREPARATION TIME: 20 MINUTES

GREEN PEA GUACAMOLE
¾ cup (100 g) shelled fresh green peas
1 ripe avocado, peeled and pitted
Juice of 1½ limes
2 tablespoons extra virgin olive oil
1 small shallot, minced
½ red chile, seeded and minced
6 cilantro sprigs, leaves only, finely chopped
Salt and pepper, to taste

2 kaiser rolls, split
½ cup (20 g) lamb's lettuce (mâche) or other small-leaf lettuce
4 ounces (120 g) hot-smoked salmon
¼ cucumber, seeded and julienned
Handful of microgreens

Fill a bowl with ice water. Bring a small saucepan of water to a boil. Cook the peas for 6 to 9 minutes, until tender. Scoop them out of the pan with a skimmer and transfer them immediately to the ice water to cool. Drain, then pat dry with a kitchen towel.

Mash the avocado and peas with a fork in a small bowl. Mix in the lime juice, olive oil, shallot, chile, and cilantro. Season with salt and pepper.

Spread the guacamole on the cut sides of the rolls and scatter on the lettuce. Pull the salmon apart and divide it between the rolls. Top with cucumber and microgreens, season with salt and pepper, and serve.

CALORIES 662 —— FAT 41 G —— SAT FAT 6 G —— CARBS 55 G
SUGARS 13 G —— PROTEIN 25 G —— SODIUM 773 MG —— FIBER 9 G

FRITTO MISTO
& Salsa Roja

In France it's known as petite friture, in Italy fritto misto: little fried fish to enjoy with drinks or as an appetizer. My fritto features not only fish, but also a generous serving of fresh vegetables.

SERVES 2
PREPARATION TIME: 45 MINUTES

BATTER

1⅓ cups (160 g) all-purpose flour
Generous ¾ cup (200 ml) beer or
  sparkling water
1½ teaspoons baking powder
1 teaspoon honey
Salt, to taste

SALSA ROJA

3 medium tomatoes, seeded and
  diced
½ red onion, finely chopped
1 garlic clove, finely chopped
1 jalapeño, seeded and finely
  chopped
6 cilantro sprigs, leaves only, finely
  chopped
1 tablespoon extra virgin olive oil
Pepper, to taste

Oil, for frying
10 okra pods, trimmed
2 to 3 ounces (50 g) green beans,
  trimmed
10 green asparagus spears, woody
  ends removed
½ medium zucchini, sliced into
  ¼-inch (6 mm) rounds
7 ounces (200 g) smelts
½ lemon, cut into wedges, for
  serving

To make the batter, whisk together the flour, beer, baking powder, and honey in a large bowl. Add a pinch of salt. Chill in the fridge for 30 minutes.

To make the salsa, combine the tomatoes, onion, garlic, jalapeño, cilantro (reserve some for garnish), and olive oil in a small bowl. Season with salt and chill in the fridge until you're ready to serve.

Take the batter out of the fridge. Place a heavy-bottomed pan over medium-high heat and pour in about 1½ inches (4 cm) of oil. Heat the oil to 350°F (180°C).

Dip the okra, beans, asparagus, zucchini, and fish into the batter, one piece at a time. Fry for 1 to 2 minutes until golden brown, in small batches so the oil stays at a constant temperature. Remove with a skimmer and drain on paper towels to absorb excess oil.

Serve with the salsa roja and lemon wedges.

CALORIES 779 —— FAT 32 G —— SAT FAT 5 G —— CARBS 89 G
SUGARS 18 G —— PROTEIN 31 G —— SODIUM 309 MG —— FIBER 9 G

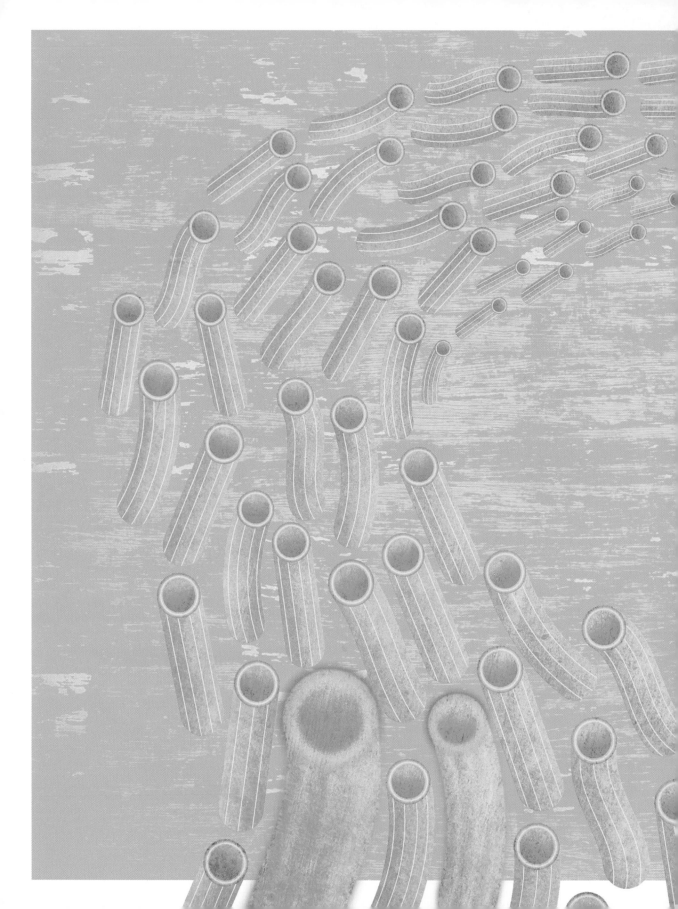

PASTA, PIZZA & NOODLES

SPAGHETTI CARBONARA
WITH SPINACH, DULSE & SMOKED
SALMON — 131

TOMATO & TUNA
GNOCCHETTI — 132

PASTA AL FORNO
WITH KALE & MUSHROOMS — 135

ASPARAGUS & LOBSTER
LASAGNA — 136

PUFF PASTRY PIZZA
WITH TUNA TAPENADE, ARTICHOKE &
CHARD — 141

FETTUCCINE PISTOU
WITH SEA LAVENDER, TURNIP
GREENS & BAY SCALLOPS — 142

FIDEUÀ CADAQUÉS
WITH ROMANO BEANS, BELL PEPPER
& TIGER PRAWNS — 145

ORZO, MARSH SAMPHIRE & FENNEL
WITH LOBSTER — 147

BUTTERNUT SQUASH GNOCCHI
WITH ROASTED TOMATOES &
LANGOUSTINES — 148

RAVIOLI
WITH LEEK, RICOTTA &
WOLFFISH — 151

Pasta is the ideal vehicle for veggies and fish; the combinations are truly endless. Here you'll find recipes for quick weekday meals and for more elaborate dinners, too. Too much pasta? Take inspiration from the tips on page 132 and give your leftovers a fresh twist the next day.

SPAGHETTI CARBONARA
with Spinach, Dulse & Smoked Salmon

This is my veggies-and-fish take on pasta carbonara. I'm using spinach and dulse, a red seaweed that has a salty flavor similar to bacon after cooking. It's delicious with this rich sauce made with cream, egg, Parmesan, and the cooking liquid from the vegetables.

SERVES 2
PREPARATION TIME: 25 MINUTES

Salt and pepper, to taste
8 ounces (225 g) spaghetti
Light olive oil, for frying
1 cup (100 g) coarsely chopped cremini mushrooms
1 shallot, minced
1 garlic clove, minced
1 tablespoon dried dulse
10 cups (300 g) baby spinach
2 eggs
⅓ cup (30 g) grated Parmesan
2 tablespoons light cream
3 to 4 ounces (100 g) cold-smoked wild sockeye salmon, coarsely chopped (see Tip)
4 chives, finely chopped

TIP: The wild sockeye salmon can be swapped out for smoked farmed salmon.

Bring a medium saucepan of salted water to a boil. Cook the spaghetti according to the package directions, until al dente.

Meanwhile, heat the oil in a large frying pan over medium-high heat. Sauté the mushrooms until golden brown, 3 to 4 minutes. Add the shallot and garlic and fry until softened, 1 to 2 minutes. Add the dulse and cook until lightly softened, 1 minute. Stir in the spinach until wilted, 2 to 3 minutes. Lower the heat.

Drain the spaghetti, reserving about 1 cup (240 ml) of the pasta cooking water. Add the spaghetti to the mushroom-spinach mixture. Remove the pan from the heat.

Beat the eggs, Parmesan, and cream together in a bowl. Stir in 1 tablespoon of the pasta water (make sure the liquid has cooled slightly so the egg doesn't scramble).

Stir the egg-cheese mixture into the spaghetti; mix well so all the strands are properly coated. Add a bit more of the pasta water if the sauce is too thick. Finally, fold in the salmon and chives. Season with pepper.

CALORIES 760 —— FAT 23 G —— SAT FAT 8 G —— CARBS 97 G
SUGARS 7 G —— PROTEIN 42 G —— SODIUM 844 MG —— FIBER 7 G

TOMATO & TUNA GNOCCHETTI

Shortly after the start of the COVID-19 pandemic, celebrated Italian chef Massimo Bottura launched a fantastic daily cooking show on Instagram. One of his ideas? Cook something today and use the leftovers in another dish tomorrow. This pasta with tomato and tuna sauce serves two, with enough to also make the recipe on page 135.

SERVES 2, PLUS EXTRA FOR
ANOTHER DISH
PREPARATION TIME: 30 MINUTES

Salt and pepper, to taste
16 ounces (455 g) gnocchetti
    sardi, or other small pasta shape
Extra virgin olive oil
2 shallots, finely chopped
1 red chile, seeded and finely
    chopped
2 garlic cloves, finely chopped
3 salted anchovy fillets, soaked to
    remove excess salt and drained
2 tablespoons white wine
4 cups (600 g) cherry tomatoes
2 tablespoons capers, rinsed and
    drained
2 teaspoons red wine vinegar
2 rosemary sprigs
2 thyme sprigs
Three 5-ounce (142 g) cans of
    tuna, drained
2 basil sprigs, leaves only

Bring a medium saucepan of salted water to a boil and cook the pasta according to the package directions, until al dente.

Meanwhile, heat a splash of olive oil in a large frying pan over medium-high heat and cook the shallots and chile until softened, 1 minute. Add the garlic and anchovies and stir until the anchovies have melted, 1 to 2 minutes. Deglaze the pan with the wine before adding the tomatoes, capers, vinegar, rosemary, and thyme. Lower the heat, cover, and simmer for 10 minutes to allow the flavors to combine.

Remove the rosemary and thyme sprigs from the sauce. Fold in the tuna.

Drain the pasta and add to the pan with the tomato-tuna sauce.

Garnish with the basil, drizzle with some olive oil, and finish with freshly ground pepper.

CALORIES 670 —— FAT 21 G —— SAT FAT 3 G —— CARBS 80 G
SUGARS 8 G —— PROTEIN 35 G —— SODIUM 800 MG

PASTA AL FORNO
with Kale & Mushrooms

The recipe on page 132 forms the basis of this oven dish. I've added extra ingredients like Tuscan kale, mushrooms, and mozzarella. It's a quick and easy way to turn yesterday's leftovers into a new and different-tasting meal.

SERVES 2
PREPARATION TIME: 40 MINUTES

½ recipe Tomato & Tuna
   Gnocchetti (page 132)
Light olive oil
2½ cups (250 g) quartered cremini
   mushrooms
2 tablespoons dry sherry
Salt and pepper, to taste
One 14-ounce (400 g) can whole
   peeled plum tomatoes
2 cups (150 g) coarsely chopped
   Tuscan kale leaves
7 ounces (200 g) fresh mozzarella,
   sliced
1 cup (100 g) grated Parmesan

Preheat the oven to 400°F (200°C).

Warm the leftover pasta and sauce with 1 tablespoon of water in a large pot over low heat until lukewarm. Don't let it boil; you only need to warm it through so it's easier to mix in the new ingredients.

Heat 1 tablespoon oil in a medium frying pan over high heat and sauté the mushrooms until golden brown, 8 to 10 minutes. Deglaze with the sherry and season with salt and pepper. Stir the mushrooms into the pasta.

Mash the tomatoes with a potato masher, but make sure they retain some texture. Add to the pasta, along with their juices and the kale. Season again with salt and pepper, if you like.

Grease a baking dish with olive oil. Spoon the pasta mixture into the pan and dot with the mozzarella slices. Sprinkle the Parmesan on top. Bake for 15 to 20 minutes, until everything is heated through. Serve immediately.

CALORIES 1,322 —— FAT 58 G —— SAT FAT 13 G —— CARBS 116 G
SUGAR 25 G —— PROTEIN 80 G —— SODIUM 2,049 MG —— FIBER 9 G

ASPARAGUS & LOBSTER LASAGNA

This is my friend Inge Tichelaar's favorite recipe. She did the food styling for this book and is a huge fan of Italian cuisine. Buon appetito!

SERVES 2
PREPARATION TIME: 1 HOUR

8 white asparagus spears, woody
    ends removed
Salt and pepper, to taste
4 dried lasagna sheets
One 17- to 21-ounce (500 to 600 g)
    lobster, cooked, shelled, and torn
    into large chunks (see page 147)
1 cup (120 g) grated pecorino

BÉCHAMEL SAUCE
3 tablespoons butter
½ cup (60 g) all-purpose flour
2 cups (500 ml) milk
10 tarragon sprigs, leaves only,
    finely chopped

Preheat the oven to 350°F (180°C).

Cut ¾ inch (2 cm) off the bottom of the asparagus spears and place the ends in a saucepan. Double-peel the asparagus by dragging a vegetable peeler from top to bottom, all the way around, then repeating the process. Add the peels to the pan with the ends. Add 4 cups (1 L) of water and bring to a boil.

Place the asparagus spears in a saucepan big enough for them to lie side by side without overlapping. Pour the boiling water and trimmings over the asparagus. Add a pinch of salt and cover with a kitchen towel to keep the asparagus submerged, making sure the towel is completely tucked inside the pan and doesn't hang over the sides. Bring to a boil and cook for 4 minutes. Turn off the heat and leave the asparagus in the pan, under the towel, for another 10 minutes, to finish cooking. The asparagus is done when you can slip the tip of a knife into the bottom with ease. Drain the asparagus spears (discard the ends and peelings) and pat dry with a clean towel.

Meanwhile, bring a large pot of salted water to a boil. Add the lasagna sheets and cook for 5 minutes, until al dente. Make sure the sheets don't clump together. Drain and rinse under cold water to stop the cooking process. Lay them out separately (not overlapping) on parchment paper.

To make the béchamel sauce, melt the butter in a small saucepan over low heat. Whisk in the flour. Gradually pour in the milk, whisking constantly until you have a smooth sauce. Simmer, whisking occasionally, until the sauce thickens. Add the tarragon and season with salt and pepper.

Coat the bottom of an 11 x 7-inch (30 x 20 cm) baking dish with a thin layer of béchamel sauce and cover it with the lasagna sheets. Arrange the asparagus on top of the pasta, followed by another layer of sauce, and then the pieces of lobster. Finish with the rest of the béchamel and sprinkle with the pecorino. Bake for 10 to 15 minutes, until the top has nicely browned.

CALORIES 923 — FAT 43 G — SAT FAT 26 G — CARBS 80 G
SUGARS 16 G — PROTEIN 51 G — SODIUM 1,272 MG — FIBER 2 G

PUFF PASTRY PIZZA
with Tuna Tapenade, Artichoke & Chard

Tinned fish is a great addition to many vegetable dishes, as I discovered while writing this book. That's certainly true for everybody's favorite, tuna. The tapenade in this recipe is made with tuna and anchovies. Unlike most tinned fish, anchovies aren't steamed, but ripened in salt for six months before being canned with olive oil. That's why anchovies have a limited shelf life and are best kept in the fridge.

SERVES 2
PREPARATION TIME: 45 MINUTES

TUNA TAPENADE
One 5-ounce (142 g) can of tuna in olive oil, drained
½ garlic clove
3 salted anchovy fillets, soaked to remove excess salt and drained
⅔ cup (100 g) black olives, pitted
2 teaspoons capers, rinsed and drained
2 tablespoons light olive oil
2 teaspoons red wine vinegar

One 17-ounce (500 g) package of puff pastry, thawed if frozen
6 ounces (150 g) mixed tomatoes (about 2 small tomatoes), thinly sliced
¾ cup (200 g) artichoke hearts (from a can or jar), coarsely chopped
2 scallions, halved lengthwise
6 cups (200 g) Swiss chard, leaves only
2 tablespoons black olives
4 thyme sprigs
2 oregano sprigs, leaves only, finely chopped
Extra virgin olive oil
Salt and pepper, to taste
2 basil sprigs, leaves only

Preheat the oven to 350°F (180°C).

To make the tapenade, blend the tuna, garlic, anchovies, olives, capers, light olive oil, and vinegar in a food processor or with an immersion blender to form a coarse paste.

Line a baking sheet with parchment paper and preheat it in the oven. Cover the sheet with the puff pastry sheets. Lightly score a ¾-inch (2 cm) border around the edge of the pastry. Spread on the tapenade, making sure to leave the edges uncovered. Top with the tomato.

Combine the artichoke, scallion, chard, olives, thyme, and oregano in a medium bowl with 2 tablespoons of extra virgin olive oil. Season with salt and pepper. Scatter the vegetables onto the tomatoes.

Bake the pizza for 20 to 25 minutes, until the edges are golden brown. Drizzle with extra virgin olive oil and garnish with basil. Serve immediately.

CALORIES 1,324 —— FAT 91 G —— SAT FAT 33 G —— CARBS 95 G
SUGARS 10 G —— PROTEIN 35 G —— SODIUM 2,377 MG —— FIBER 10 G

FETTUCCINE PISTOU
with Sea Lavender, Turnip Greens & Bay Scallops

Pistou is an olive and basil sauce from Provence. Unlike Italian pesto, it doesn't contain pine nuts. This pasta dish is made with gorgeous green veggies, like turnip greens, and briny sea vegetables. Bay scallops, or pétoncles, which are smaller than sea scallops but equally delicious, complete the dish.

SERVES 2
PREPARATION TIME: 25 MINUTES

9 ounces (250 g) bay scallops,
 frozen or fresh
Salt and pepper, to taste

PISTOU
1 garlic clove, halved
1 oil-packed anchovy fillet, drained
2½ cups (60 g) basil leaves
¼ cup (60 ml) extra virgin olive oil
¼ cup (20 g) grated Parmesan

10 small green asparagus spears,
 woody ends removed
8 ounces (225 g) dried fettuccine
2 tablespoons light olive oil
1 garlic clove, sliced
Scant 2 cups (70 g) coarsely
 chopped sea lavender
Scant 2 cups (70 g) coarsely
 chopped turnip greens
Fresh lemon juice, to taste
4 sea fennel sprigs (optional)

If using frozen scallops, thaw them in the fridge the night before by placing them on a rack with a container underneath to catch the juices. Pat them dry with a paper towel and sprinkle with salt on both sides. Set aside.

To make the pistou, mash the garlic with the anchovy in a mortar. Add the basil a little at a time and grind until a smooth paste forms. Mix in the extra virgin olive oil, then the Parmesan. Set aside.

Bring a saucepan of salted water to a boil. Blanch the asparagus for 2 to 3 minutes, until al dente. Drain, then run under cold water to stop the cooking process. Pat dry with a kitchen towel. Set aside.

Bring a large pot of salted water to a boil. Cook the fettuccine according to package directions, until al dente.

Meanwhile, heat the light olive oil in a medium frying pan over medium-high heat. Sear the scallops until they're nicely browned on the outside, 1 to 2 minutes. Remove from the pan and set aside.

Sauté the garlic for 1 to 2 minutes in the remaining oil until fragrant. Add the sea lavender, turnip greens, and asparagus. Cook for about 1 minute, until warm.

Drain the fettuccine and transfer it to a large bowl with the sea lavender, turnip greens, and asparagus. Stir in the pistou. Season to taste with lemon juice and pepper. Fold in the scallops.

Serve the pasta from the bowl or divide it between two plates. Garnish with the sea fennel (if using).

CALORIES 958 —— FAT 50 G —— SAT FAT 10 G —— CARBS 87 G
SUGARS 2 G —— PROTEIN 45 G —— SODIUM 807 MG —— FIBER 6 G

FIDEUÀ CADAQUÉS
with Romano Beans, Bell Pepper & Tiger Prawns

I always have this dish at La Sirena and Can Rafa, my favorite restaurants in Cadaqués, an enchanting village in Catalonia, where I've been going for many years. Fideuà is a one-pan meal with seafood and noodles (fideo means "noodles"). Like the better-known paella, the noodles are cooked in stock in a large, shallow pan.

SERVES 4
PREPARATION TIME: 50 MINUTES

1 tablespoon light olive oil
1 yellow onion, finely chopped
1 red bell pepper, seeded and coarsely chopped
1 leek, white and light green parts only, sliced into rings
½ fennel bulb, cored and coarsely chopped
1 garlic clove, finely chopped
½ teaspoon red pepper flakes
12 ounces (350 g) tomatoes (about 4 large), seeded and cut into ¼-inch (6 mm) cubes
1¾ cups (400 ml) Vegetable or Fish Stock (page 232)
½ teaspoon saffron threads
10 ounces (300 g) fideos or vermicelli, broken into 1½-inch (4 cm) pieces
10 shell-on tiger prawns, heads removed, deveined
3 to 4 ounces (100 g) Romano or other flat beans, sliced diagonally
1 lemon, quartered, for serving

Preheat the oven to 400°F (200°C).

Heat the oil in a large, wide oven-safe frying pan over medium-high heat. Add the onion, bell pepper, leek, fennel, and garlic and sweat, for 2 to 3 minutes, stirring constantly; you want the vegetables to soften but not brown. Sprinkle in the red pepper flakes and cook for 1 minute. Add the tomatoes, lower the heat, and cook for 10 minutes, stirring occasionally, until the tomatoes break down.

Add the stock and saffron and stir for 2 to 3 minutes, so all the ingredients are properly combined. Arrange the fideos over the pan and press them into the sauce—no more stirring from now on! Cook uncovered for 6 minutes to let the flavors blend. Scatter the prawns and beans on top and press them into the pasta. The fideuà is done as soon as the noodles "stand up," about 12 minutes after adding them to the pan.

Place the pan in the oven for 2 minutes to lightly caramelize the top.

Serve with the lemon wedges.

TIP: It's best to use an oven-safe paella pan or wide frying pan for this dish, so all the ingredients are close to the heat source.

CALORIES 355 —— FAT 7 G —— SAT FAT 2 G —— CARBS 58 G
SUGARS 8 G —— PROTEIN 17 G —— SODIUM 101 MG —— FIBER 7 G

ORZO, MARSH SAMPHIRE & FENNEL with Lobster

Orzo is a dried pasta that closely resembles rice in both shape and size. It's usually prepared in much the same way as a risotto, in a broth. In this case, I'm using homemade lobster stock, flavored with tomato and other vegetables. The aniseed flavor of the fennel pairs really well with the shellfish.

SERVES 2
ADVANCE PREPARATION TIME: 1 HOUR
PREPARATION TIME: 45 MINUTES

One 17- to 21-ounce (500 to 600 g) live lobster
Oil, for frying
1 yellow onion, coarsely chopped
1 leek, white and light green parts only, coarsely chopped
1 celery stalk, coarsely chopped
1 carrot, peeled and coarsely chopped
½ fennel bulb, cored and coarsely chopped (save the fronds)
2 tablespoons tomato paste
2 bay leaves
1 teaspoon piment d'espelette or red pepper flakes
1 star anise
3 tablespoons brandy
Scant ½ cup (100 ml) white wine
2 generous cups (500 ml) Fish Stock (page 232)
Salt and pepper, to taste
Generous ½ cup (125 g) orzo
2 medium tomatoes, seeded and diced
1½ cups (60 g) marsh samphire
1½ tablespoons butter

Place the lobster in the freezer for 1 hour to stun it.

Bring a large pot with enough water to cover the lobster to a boil over high heat. Cut the lobster's head in half with a large chef's knife. Place the lobster in the boiling water, headfirst, and immediately put the lid on. Cook the lobster for about 5 minutes, until tender. Scoop the lobster out with a skimmer, drain, and set aside to cool.

Break off the tail, crack the shell, and remove the meat. Pull off the claws, crack them, and remove the meat with a lobster pick. Coarsely chop the tail and claw meat and set them aside. Coarsely chop the shells, head and body, and swimmerets.

Heat 3 tablespoons oil in a heavy-bottomed pan. Sauté the shells, head, body, and swimmerets for 3 to 4 minutes over high heat, stirring constantly, until fragrant. Add the onion, leek, celery, carrot, and fennel and sauté until softened, 5 minutes. Add the tomato paste and cook for 2 minutes to lower the acidity. Add the bay leaves, piment d'espelette, and star anise and stir well. Deglaze with the brandy and pour in the white wine. Boil for 1 minute before adding the fish stock. Simmer uncovered over low heat to let the flavors blend, about 25 minutes.

Remove the star anise from the pan, and using a potato masher, crush the lobster shells. Strain the mixture through a fine sieve and discard the solids. Season the stock with salt and pepper.

Heat a generous splash of oil in a large frying pan and sauté the orzo over medium-high heat until it browns, about 4 minutes. Pour in the lobster stock, mix well, and simmer until the orzo is al dente, 12 to 15 minutes. Stir in the tomatoes and marsh samphire. Finally, add the chunks of lobster and fold in the butter. Season with salt and pepper, if you like. Garnish with the fennel fronds.

CALORIES 733 —— FAT 32 G —— SAT FAT 9 G —— CARBS 63 G
SUGARS 8 G —— PROTEIN 30 G —— SODIUM 921 MG —— FIBER 6 G

BUTTERNUT SQUASH GNOCCHI
with Roasted Tomatoes & Langoustines

These gnocchi are made with butternut squash instead of potato. The tomatoes are slow-roasted in the oven with thyme, rosemary, and garlic. Delicious with langoustines, but equally so with lobster or crab. Fried sage leaves pair really well with the flavors in this dish.

SERVES 4
PREPARATION TIME: 1 HOUR

1 small butternut squash (about
    2 pounds/1 kg)
2 garlic cloves, peeled
12 cherry tomatoes, halved
6 tablespoons extra virgin olive oil
Salt and pepper, to taste
1 rosemary sprig
1 thyme sprig
1 teaspoon smoked paprika
1 teaspoon ground turmeric
1⅔ cups (200 g) all-purpose flour,
    plus extra for dusting
1 egg, beaten
1 teaspoon red pepper flakes
4 langoustines, halved lengthwise
3 sage sprigs, leaves only

Preheat the oven to 350°F (180°C).

Halve the squash, remove the seeds, and cut the squash into big chunks (leave the skin on). Line a baking sheet with parchment paper and arrange the squash on it. Bake for 30 minutes, until softened. Remove from the oven and set aside to cool. Lower the oven temperature to 250°F (120°C).

Coarsely chop 1 garlic clove. In a baking dish, combine the chopped garlic with the tomatoes, 3 tablespoons of the olive oil, and the rosemary and thyme. Season with salt and pepper. Roast the tomatoes in the oven for 10 minutes, until softened. Remove from the oven and discard the thyme, rosemary, and garlic.

Scoop the flesh out of the squash skin and purée it in a food processor. Transfer to a bowl. Stir in the paprika, turmeric, a pinch of salt, and the flour and egg. Mix well, making sure to get rid of any lumps. Scatter some extra flour on a plate. Using two teaspoons, shape the squash mixture into little balls and dredge them in the flour. Set the gnocchi aside.

Bring a medium saucepan of salted water to a boil and add the gnocchi. They're done as soon as they rise to the surface. Scoop out the gnocchi with a skimmer and drain them well before transferring them to a bowl. Gently coat them with 1 tablespoon of olive oil.

Thinly slice the remaining garlic clove. Heat the remaining 2 tablespoons of olive oil in a large frying pan over medium-high heat. Sauté the garlic and red pepper flakes until softened, stirring constantly, 1 to 2 minutes. Increase the heat and add the langoustines, frying them in the aromatic oil until warmed and lightly colored, 1 to 2 minutes. Remove the langoustines from the pan and fry the sage leaves in the oil until crisp, about 1 minute.

Divide the tomatoes between two plates and add the gnocchi. Top with the langoustines, drizzle with the aromatic oil from the pan, and garnish with the sage leaves.

CALORIES 513 — FAT 23 G — SAT FAT 4 G — CARBS 67 G
SUGAR 7 G — PROTEIN 14 G — SODIUM 73 MG — FIBER 2 G

RAVIOLI
with Leek, Ricotta & Wolffish

During one of many dinners at my good friend Tonin Vukaj's house, I had this extraordinary ravioli dish. Not difficult to make, and the combination of white fish, creamy ricotta, and fragrant thyme is unforgettable. If you can't get wolffish, you can use any whitefish, such as cod or haddock, instead.

SERVES 2
PREPARATION TIME: 90 MINUTES

RAVIOLI SHEETS (SEE TIP)
3⅓ cups (400 g) type "oo" flour
Scant ⅔ cup (100 g) semolina flour
5 large eggs

Extra virgin olive oil
2 leeks, white and light green parts
   only, sliced
1 garlic clove, peeled
1 tablespoon white wine
5 ounces (150 g) skinless wolffish
   fillet, finely chopped
Scant 1 cup (200 g) ricotta
Juice of ¼ lemon
Salt and pepper, to taste
1 egg yolk, beaten
4 tablespoons butter

> **TIP**: Pressed for time? You can use wonton wrappers instead of making your own dough. You'll need about 10 wrappers.

To make the ravioli, combine the "oo" and semolina flours in a large bowl. Transfer the mixture to a flat work surface and make a well in the middle. Crack the eggs into the well and whisk them together with a fork, then slowly whisk in the flour. Once all of the flour is incorporated, knead for about 10 minutes, until the dough is firm and elastic. Wrap in a damp kitchen towel and let rest in the fridge for 45 minutes.

Meanwhile, heat 1 tablespoon of olive oil in a medium frying pan over medium-high heat. Add the leek, then stick the garlic clove on a fork and stir the leek with it until the leek starts to soften, about 1 minute. Discard the garlic. Add the white wine and braise the leek uncovered over low heat until soft, 3 to 4 minutes. Transfer to a medium bowl and let cool.

Heat another 1 tablespoon olive oil in the pan. Add the wolffish and cook until tender, 2 to 3 minutes, flipping once halfway through. Drain on a paper towel, then add to the bowl with the leek. Add the ricotta and mix well. Season with the lemon juice and salt and pepper.

Roll out the dough into four thin sheets, each about 20 inches (50 cm) long and 4 inches (10 cm) wide. Drop the fish mixture, about 1 tablespoon at a time, in a line about ¼ inch (6 mm) off-center on one sheet, making sure to keep ¼ inch (6 mm) of space around each pile of filling on all sides. Brush the edges of the dough sheet with egg yolk. Place another sheet over the filling, and gently press the dough together, pressing out as much air as possible. Use a 2-inch (5 cm) cookie cutter or glass to cut the dough around the filling into individual ravioli. Gently remove the excess dough, then crimp the edges of the ravioli with a fork. Set the ravioli aside on a sheet of parchment paper. Repeat with the remaining dough sheets and the remaining filling. You should have about 8 to 10 ravioli total.

Bring a large pot of salted water to a boil. Add the ravioli, in batches if necessary, and cook until they float to the surface, 3 to 4 minutes. Scoop out the ravioli with a skimmer and drain on a kitchen towel.

Melt the butter in a large frying pan. Toss the ravioli in the butter and gently warm through for 2 to 3 minutes. Season with salt and pepper and serve.

CALORIES 1,746 —— FAT 69 G —— SAT FAT 30 G —— CARBS 207 G
SUGAR 11 G —— PROTEIN 70 G —— SODIUM 543 MG —— FIBER 10 G

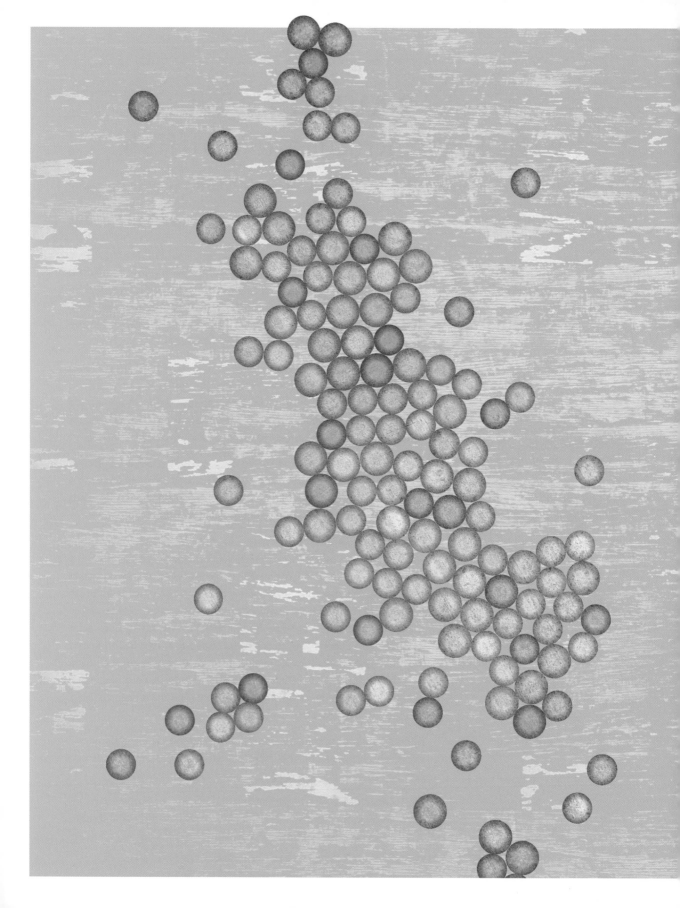

GRAINS & LEGUMES

COUSCOUS
WITH VEGETABLES & CHERMOULA
SWORDFISH — 155

TABBOULEH SALAD
WITH SEA BASS & HARISSA
YOGURT — 156

KHICHDI
WITH VEGETABLES & HADDOCK — 159

QUINOA SALAD
WITH SEA BASS &
CHIMICHURRI — 160

RISOTTO
WITH LEEK, FENNEL &
RAZOR CLAMS — 164

PESCE IN SAOR
WITH ISRAELI COUSCOUS — 167

RED LENTILS
WITH ROASTED BELL PEPPER &
WHITING — 168

As someone schooled in the classic Mediterranean kitchen, it's taken me a while to start cooking more extensively with grains and legumes. But my extensive travels and the influences of Middle Eastern cuisine, especially, have opened up a whole new (food) world for me. This chapter provides inspiration for vegetable and fish dishes based around ingredients like couscous, bulgur wheat, and quinoa.

COUSCOUS
with Vegetables & Chermoula Swordfish

In this recipe, swordfish is marinated in chermoula, an herb and spice mixture used to season fish in Morocco, where every family has its own recipe. For an extra flavor boost, the vegetables are braised in the same spice blend. The fish and vegetables are delicious mixed with steamed couscous.

SERVES 2
PREPARATION TIME: 1 HOUR

CHERMOULA
1 teaspoon cumin seeds
1 tablespoon coriander seeds
1 tablespoon ground cinnamon
1 teaspoon smoked paprika
Salt, to taste
2 garlic cloves, halved
1 green chile, seeded and finely chopped
Zest and juice of 1 lemon
⅓ cup (80 ml) light olive oil
1 bunch of cilantro, finely chopped
½ bunch of flat-leaf parsley, finely chopped

1 swordfish steak (9 ounces/250 g), skin removed
Extra virgin olive oil
1 garlic clove, minced
1 bell pepper, seeded, coarsely chopped
½ eggplant, coarsely chopped
6 cherry tomatoes, halved
½ medium butternut squash, peeled and finely chopped
1 cup (150 g) canned chickpeas, rinsed and drained
Scant 1 cup (150 g) raw couscous (not instant)
2 cups (500 ml) Vegetable Stock (page 232)
Zest and juice of 1 lemon
Pepper, to taste
2 cilantro sprigs, leaves only, coarsely chopped
1 mint sprig, leaves only, finely chopped
¼ cup (65 g) full-fat plain yogurt

To make the chermoula, grind the cumin and coriander seeds in a mortar and mix in the cinnamon, paprika, and a pinch of salt. Add the garlic and chile and pound until a smooth paste forms. Transfer to a medium bowl. Add the lemon zest and juice, followed by the olive oil, cilantro, and parsley, and stir to combine. Rub the swordfish on both sides with half of the chermoula, cover, and let it marinate at room temperature for 30 minutes.

Heat 1 tablespoon of olive oil in a large frying pan over medium-high heat and sweat the garlic for 1 to 2 minutes. Spoon in 1 tablespoon of the remaining chermoula and heat through. Add the bell pepper, eggplant, tomatoes, and squash to the pan and cook until softened, 4 minutes. Lower the heat and gently simmer the vegetables, until well cooked and soft, 20 to 30 minutes. Stir in the chickpeas after about 15 minutes. Add a splash of water if the mixture becomes too dry.

Meanwhile, place the couscous into a bowl and add a pinch of salt. Drizzle with 1 tablespoon of olive oil and 1 tablespoon of cold water and work into the couscous with your fingers until coated.

Bring the stock to a boil in a medium saucepan. Place the couscous in a sieve or steamer over the liquid, cover, and steam until al dente, 10 to 12 minutes. Transfer the couscous to a large bowl and fluff with a fork or whisk. Season with the lemon juice and zest, 2 tablespoons of olive oil, and salt and pepper.

Heat a grill pan over high heat and grill the swordfish 2 to 3 minutes on each side, until crunchy on the outside and tender inside. Carefully transfer the fish to a plate, cover with aluminum foil, and let cook in the residual heat for another 4 to 5 minutes. Cut the fish into bite-size pieces and fold them, together with the vegetables, into the couscous.

Serve the couscous on a platter and garnish with the cilantro. Mix the mint and yogurt in a small bowl and serve on the side.

CALORIES 1,059 —— FAT 44 G —— SAT FAT 7G —— CARBS 128 G
SUGARS 21 G —— PROTEIN 47 G —— SODIUM 403 MG —— FIBER 18 G

TABBOULEH SALAD
with Sea Bass & Harissa Yogurt

Tabbouleh is a wonderful, fresh-tasting bulgur salad with tomatoes, mint, parsley, and various other herbs and spices. The sea bass fillets turn this side dish from the Lebanese kitchen into an entrée in its own right. Fry the bass skin side down first to make it extra crispy.

SERVES 2
PREPARATION TIME: 40 MINUTES

½ cup (70 g) fine bulgur wheat
Scant ⅓ cup (70 ml) of boiling
    water (optional)
1 tablespoon pine nuts

HARISSA YOGURT SAUCE
¼ cup (65 g) full-fat plain yogurt
Zest and juice of ½ lemon
1 tablespoon harissa (preferably
    green)
1 tablespoon extra virgin olive oil
Salt and pepper, to taste

1 bunch of flat-leaf parsley, leaves
    only, very finely chopped
½ bunch of mint, finely chopped
2 medium tomatoes, seeded,
    finely diced
½ small red onion, finely chopped
2 scallions, finely chopped
1 teaspoon ground cumin
1 tablespoon pomegranate
    molasses
Juice of 1 lemon
Extra virgin olive oil
2 skin-on sea bass fillets
    (3 ounces/90 g each)
Oil, for frying

Prepare the bulgur according to package directions. Or place the bulgur in a bowl and pour over a scant ⅓ cup (70 ml) of boiling water. Cover and let stand for 20 minutes, until al dente. Fluff the bulgur with a fork and let cool.

Meanwhile, toast the pine nuts in a dry frying pan over medium-high heat until golden brown, 2 to 3 minutes. Transfer to a plate and let cool.

To make the sauce, mix the yogurt, lemon zest and juice, harissa, and olive oil in a small bowl. Season with salt and pepper. Set aside.

Combine the cooled bulgur in a medium bowl with the parsley, mint, tomatoes, onion, scallions, and cumin. Add the pomegranate molasses, lemon juice, and 2 to 3 tablespoons of olive oil and mix well. Season with salt and pepper.

Season the sea bass fillets with salt on both sides. Heat 1 tablespoon oil in a frying pan over medium-high heat. Fry the fillets skin side down for 2 to 3 minutes without moving them, until the skin is crispy. Flip them and fry 1 to 2 minutes more. Remove from the pan, cut into bite-size pieces, and let cool.

Spoon the bulgur onto a plate or into a bowl and top with the fish. Scatter over the pine nuts. Drizzle with the harissa yogurt. Serve the remaining sauce on the side.

CALORIES 476 —— FAT 22 G —— SAT FAT 4 G —— CARBS 51 G
SUGAR 15 G —— PROTEIN 26 G —— SODIUM 172 MG —— FIBER 11 G

KHICHDI
with Vegetables & Haddock

Khichdi is a seasoned rice and lentil dish that originates in India. The British put their own spin on it by replacing the lentils with fish and adding a garnish of hard-boiled eggs.

SERVES 2
PREPARATION TIME: 1 HOUR

1 medium yellow onion, coarsely chopped
1 medium zucchini, coarsely chopped
2 green asparagus spears, woody ends removed, coarsely chopped
½ medium eggplant, coarsely chopped
2 tablespoons sunflower oil
1 teaspoon curry powder
½ teaspoon ground turmeric
¼ teaspoon grated nutmeg
Salt and pepper, to taste
1 tablespoon butter
¾-inch (2 cm) piece of ginger, peeled and finely chopped
½ red chile, seeded and finely chopped
1 garlic clove, finely chopped
⅔ cup (130 g) white basmati rice, rinsed
2 skin-on haddock fillets (4 to 5 ounces/120 to 150 g each), coarsely chopped
2 cups (500 ml) milk
2 bay leaves
6 black peppercorns
2 eggs
Juice of ¼ lemon
2 flat-leaf parsley sprigs, leaves only, coarsely chopped

Preheat the oven to 375°F (190°C).

Mix the onion, zucchini, asparagus, and eggplant with the oil in a medium bowl. Stir in the curry powder, turmeric, nutmeg, and a pinch of salt. Arrange the vegetables on a baking sheet and bake until tender and starting to char, 30 to 40 minutes.

Meanwhile, melt the butter in a medium saucepan and sweat the ginger, chile, and garlic until softened but not browned, about 2 minutes. Add the rice and a pinch of salt and stir well. Add enough cold water to cover the rice so it comes up to your second knuckle. Bring to a boil, then simmer, covered, over low heat until tender, 8 minutes. Turn off the heat and let the rice sit, covered, for another 5 minutes. Fluff the rice with a fork. If it seems too dry, you can add some of the milk the fish was cooked in (below). Keep the rice warm.

Place the haddock, milk, bay leaves, and peppercorns in a small saucepan. Bring to a boil over medium-high heat, then immediately turn off the heat. Let the fish sit in the hot milk for 6 minutes, then remove the fish and set it aside. The fish should start to fall apart when pressed.

Bring enough water to cover the eggs to a boil in a small pot. Add the eggs and cook for 7 minutes, until slightly hard-boiled. Cool the eggs under cold running water, peel, and cut into quarters.

Transfer the roasted vegetables to a large bowl, along with the aromatic oil from the baking sheet. Stir in the rice. Fold in the haddock.

Transfer the khichdi to a serving dish. Drizzle with the lemon juice and sprinkle with the parsley, salt, and freshly ground pepper. Top with the eggs.

CALORIES 725 — FAT 28 G — SAT FAT 8 G — CARBS 73 G
SUGARS 12 G — PROTEIN 43 G — SODIUM 253 MG — FIBER 8 G

QUINOA SALAD
with Sea Bass & Chimichurri

After I traveled to Peru, I got inspired to cook with quinoa more often. Quinoa is a seed with a nutty taste that originates in the Andes Mountains. It's a good substitute for grains and is available in different colors, such as white, red, brown, and black. It pairs well with all kinds of crunchy vegetables and is delicious with a pan-fried fillet of fish and my take on chimichurri, a spicy green sauce of Argentinian origin. This is one of the dishes I regularly cook for a light but nutritional meal.

SERVES 2
PREPARATION TIME: 30 MINUTES

CHIMICHURRI
2 red chiles, halved lengthwise and seeded
Extra virgin olive oil
1 tablespoon tomato paste
8 garlic cloves, coarsely chopped
2 teaspoons black peppercorns
1 teaspoon coarse salt
5 flat-leaf parsley sprigs
6 oil-packed anchovy fillets, drained
2 teaspoons fresh oregano leaves
2 teaspoons red wine vinegar

2 cups (300 g) cubed peeled butternut squash, in ½-inch (13 mm) cubes
2 cups (200 g) Romanesco florets
1 medium bell pepper, diced
Salt and pepper, to taste
½ cup (100 g) quinoa (I used black quinoa, but you can use any color you like)
1 packed cup (50 g) baby spinach
2 flat-leaf parsley sprigs, leaves only, coarsely chopped
Zest and juice of ¼ lemon

2 skin-on sea bass fillets (4 to 5 ounces/120 to 150 g each)
Oil, for frying

To make the chimichurri, bring a small saucepan full of water to a boil and then lower the heat to a simmer. Add the chiles and cook until softened, about 5 minutes. Drain, pat dry with a kitchen towel, and scrape the flesh from the skin with a teaspoon. Set the flesh aside in a small bowl.

Heat a splash of olive oil in a small frying pan over medium heat. Cook the tomato paste over low heat to remove the acidity, stirring constantly, for 1 minute. Place the garlic, peppercorns, and salt in a mortar and pound to a thick paste. Add the chile flesh, parsley, anchovies, and oregano and pound until smooth. Add the tomato paste and vinegar and mix thoroughly. Transfer to a serving bowl and set aside.

Heat 2 tablespoons oil in a large frying pan over medium-high heat. Add the squash, Romanesco, and bell pepper and season with salt and pepper. Cover and sweat until soft and cooked through, about 20 minutes, stirring occasionally. Add a splash of water if the vegetables get too dry. Transfer the vegetables to a large bowl.

Rinse the quinoa, place it in a small saucepan, and cover with plenty of cold water. Bring to a boil, then simmer over low heat for about 12 minutes, until the little tails unfurl. Drain the quinoa and return it to the pan to steam-dry.

Add the quinoa to the vegetables and stir in the spinach, parsley, and lemon zest and juice. Add a splash of olive oil and season with salt and pepper.

Season both sides of the sea bass fillets with salt. Heat 2 tablespoons oil in a medium frying pan over medium-high heat. Fry the fillets skin side down, without moving them, until the skin is crispy, 2 to 3 minutes. Flip and fry for 1 minute on the other side, until the fish is cooked through. Don't flip the fish a second time, so the skin stays crispy.

Serve the quinoa salad with the fish fillets and chimichurri.

CALORIES 770	FAT 36 G	SAT FAT 5 G	CARBS 75 G
SUGARS 9 G	PROTEIN 46 G	SODIUM 1,556 MG	FIBER 10 G

RISOTTO
with Leek, Fennel & Razor Clams

Razor clams taste similar to the popular and more widely consumed littleneck clams. They burrow upright in the sandy seabed, which makes them difficult to harvest. But they're delicious to eat—hence this razor clam risotto. Once the clams are cooked, I cut the meat into bite-size pieces.

SERVES 2
PREPARATION TIME: 40 MINUTES

14 ounces (400 g) razor clams
3 tablespoons butter
1 leek, white and light green parts only, sliced into thin rings
½ fennel bulb, cored and finely chopped (coarsely chop and save the fronds)
1 shallot, finely chopped
1 garlic clove, finely chopped
¾ cup (150 g) risotto rice (Arborio or carnaroli)
¼ cup (60 ml) white wine
1¼ cups (300 ml) Fish Stock (page 232)
1¼ cups (300 ml) Vegetable Stock (page 232)
⅓ cup (60 g) peas (thawed frozen or cooked fresh)
2 flat-leaf parsley sprigs, leaves only, coarsely chopped
Salt and pepper, to taste
Handful of coarsely chopped wild fennel (optional)

Briefly rinse the clams under cold running water.

Place the clams side by side in a large frying pan with enough space between them so they can open. Pour 2 tablespoons of water into the pan, turn the heat to medium-high, and cover with a lid. Check to see if the clams have opened after 2 to 3 minutes. Remove them from the pan, rinse off any sand, and remove the meat from the shells. Cut the meat into 1-inch (2.5 cm) pieces (see Tip) and set it aside.

Melt half of the butter in a medium saucepan over medium-high heat and sauté the leek, fennel, and shallot until softened, 2 to 3 minutes. Add the garlic and cook for 1 minute, until fragrant. Add the rice and stir until all the grains are coated and translucent, 1 to 2 minutes. Pour in the wine and cook, stirring constantly, until it is almost absorbed. Add a generous ladle full of fish stock and stir until the liquid has been absorbed. Add more stock, alternating between fish and vegetable stock according to your preference, until the risotto is al dente, about 20 minutes. You might not need all the stock.

Add the clams, peas, parsley, and the rest of the butter and gently stir to combine. Season with salt and pepper. Garnish with the wild fennel (if using) and the fennel fronds. Let sit for 1 to 2 minutes, then serve.

TIP: I remove the dark "foot" of the razor clams and use the center area and the tip because the foot can taste slightly bitter.

CALORIES 777 —— FAT 20 G —— SAT FAT 11 G —— CARBS 100 G
SUGARS 6 G —— PROTEIN 39 G —— SODIUM 428 MG —— FIBER 7 G

PESCE IN SAOR
with Israeli Couscous

Sarde in saor is a classic Venetian dish of sweet-and-sour sardines with raisins and slow-braised onions. It's traditionally served cold but is equally good lukewarm. You can use any kind of fish instead of sardines, so I've opted for sea bass in this recipe. The sweet-and-sour onion mixture goes well with Israeli couscous.

SERVES 2
PREPARATION TIME: 45 MINUTES

Light olive oil, for frying
4 large yellow onions, sliced into rings
3 tablespoons raisins
1 tablespoon pine nuts
½ medium zucchini, diced
⅓ cup (80 ml) white wine vinegar
4 thyme sprigs, leaves only, plus extra for garnish
½ cup (75 g) Israeli couscous
2 skin-on sea bass fillets (3 ounces/90 g each)
Salt, to taste

Heat 3 tablespoons oil in a large frying pan over medium-high heat. Sweat the onions for 4 minutes, stirring constantly, so they soften but don't brown. Add the raisins, pine nuts, and zucchini, and stir until the raisins and zucchini soften and the pine nuts begin to brown, 2 minutes. Deglaze the pan with the vinegar. Add the thyme. Lower the heat and simmer, stirring occasionally, until the onions soften, about 15 to 20 minutes.

Meanwhile, bring a small saucepan of water to a boil. Cook the couscous according to package directions, then drain. Add the couscous to the vegetable mixture and stir to combine.

Score the fish fillets every inch or so and sprinkle them with salt.

Heat 1 tablespoon oil in a medium frying pan over medium-high heat. Fry the fillets, skin side down, until the skin is crispy, 2 to 3 minutes. Flip and fry for 1 to 2 minutes on the other side, until the fish is cooked through. Don't flip the fish again, so the skin stays crispy.

Transfer the onion-couscous mixture to a platter and top with the fish. Garnish with the extra thyme.

CALORIES 664 —— FAT 33 G —— SAT FAT 5 G —— CARBS 69 G
SUGARS 31 G —— PROTEIN 26 G —— SODIUM 76 MG —— FIBER 9 G

RED LENTILS
with Roasted Bell Pepper & Whiting

Red lentils have a slightly sweeter and nuttier flavor compared to other lentils. Take care when cooking them—they tend to disintegrate when overcooked.

SERVES 2
PREPARATION TIME: 1 HOUR AND
20 MINUTES

6 red bell peppers
Extra virgin olive oil
Salt and pepper, to taste
½ small butternut squash, peeled
  and seeded, cut into ¾-inch
  (2 cm) cubes
Oil, for frying
1 shallot, finely chopped
½ chile, seeded and finely
  chopped
2 garlic cloves, peeled
1 cup (250 g) canned whole
  peeled tomatoes
½ bunch of basil, leaves only (save
  some for garnish)
1 cup (200 g) red lentils
1 thyme sprig
1 bay leaf
2 skin-on whiting fillets
  (3 ounces/90 g each)
2 fresh marjoram or oregano
  sprigs, leaves only

Preheat the oven to 450°F (230°C). Line a baking sheet with parchment paper.

Arrange the bell peppers on it, drizzle with olive oil, and sprinkle with salt. Roast the peppers, turning occasionally, until their skins blister and start to turn black, 15 to 20 minutes. Remove from the oven and let cool. Reduce the oven temperature to 350°F (180°C).

Peel off the bell pepper skins and remove the seeds. Cut 4 of the peppers into big chunks and 2 into strips. Set aside separately.

Line the baking sheet with clean parchment paper and arrange the squash on it. Drizzle with olive oil and bake for 30 minutes, until caramelized and softened. Turn off the oven but leave the squash inside.

Heat 1 tablespoon oil in a frying pan over medium-high heat. Sweat the shallot and chile for 1 minute, until starting to soften. Finely chop 1 garlic clove, add it to the pan, and cook until softened, 1 minute more. Add the chunks of bell pepper (but not the strips) and the tomatoes and their juices. Simmer over low heat to allow the flavors to blend, 10 minutes. Add the basil. Purée the sauce with an immersion blender. Season with salt and pepper. Keep warm.

Halve the remaining garlic clove. Place the garlic, lentils, thyme, and bay leaf in a medium saucepan and cover with plenty of cold water. Bring to a boil, lower the heat, and cook, stirring occasionally, until the lentils are fork-tender, 18 to 22 minutes. Drain the lentils; remove and discard the thyme, garlic, and bay leaf. Keep warm.

Sprinkle both sides of the whiting with salt. Heat 1 tablespoon oil in a frying pan over medium-high heat. Fry the fish skin side down until the skin is crispy, 2 to 3 minutes. Flip and fry for 1 minute on the other side, until the fish is cooked through.

Mix the lentils with the tomato-pepper sauce, roasted pepper strips, and squash in a large bowl. Serve topped with the whiting fillets. Garnish with the marjoram.

CALORIES 820 —— FAT 25 G —— SAT FAT 4 G —— CARBS 110 G
SUGARS 18 G —— PROTEIN 47 G —— SODIUM 305 MG —— FIBER 20 G

CURRIES & STEWS

I love curry paste. While many recipes call for adding and assembling flavors throughout the cooking process, a curry paste determines the taste and character of your dish from the outset. It's cooking in a different order, you might say. Stews, on the other hand, have a slow build-up of flavor intensity.

YELLOW CURRY
with Mussels

Mussels are a firm favorite in my family. When they're steamed in a little bit of liquid (don't boil them!), the resulting briny mussel liquor adds a wonderful flavor to a stock or sauce. In this recipe, the mussels are cooked in the coconut milk, so the curry is full of mussel flavor.

SERVES 2
PREPARATION TIME: 20 MINUTES

2 pounds (1 kg) mussels
Oil, for frying
1 red onion, sliced into rings
1 lemongrass stalk, bruised
1 head of bok choy, root end trimmed, coarsely chopped
3 to 4 ounces (100 g) broccolini, florets separated, stalks coarsely chopped
2 tablespoons Yellow Curry Paste (page 234)
Generous ¾ cup (200 ml) coconut milk
2 Thai basil sprigs, leaves only
½ lime, cut into wedges

Rinse the mussels and discard any broken ones. Check those that are open by tapping them against a hard surface, like a cutting board; discard any that don't close.

Heat 1 tablespoon oil in a mussel pot or large saucepan over medium-high heat. Sweat the onion and lemongrass for 2 to 3 minutes, until the onion starts to soften. Add the bok choy and broccolini and cook for 1 minute. Add the curry paste and fry for 1 minute more, until fragrant. Add the coconut milk and stir to combine.

Increase the heat and add the mussels. Stir thoroughly and cover. Steam the mussels until they open, 3 to 5 minutes, stirring after about 2 minutes. Discard any mussels that have not fully opened.

Serve the mussels, vegetables, and sauce from the pan or in a bowl, garnished with the basil and lime wedges.

CALORIES 477 —— FAT 32 G —— SAT FAT 13 G —— CARBS 26 G
SUGARS 12 G —— PROTEIN 21 G —— SODIUM 443 MG —— FIBER 2 G

VEGETABLE STEW
with Saffron & Monkfish

Poaching is gentle cooking in a liquid at a low temperature. It's one of the best ways to prepare a delicate fish like monkfish. If a fish is overcooked, its proteins tighten and you'll see a white substance ooze out and collect on the surface. The potatoes and vegetables in this stew, an abstract take on bouillabaisse, need longer cooking than the fish.

SERVES 2
ADVANCE PREPARATION TIME:
30 MINUTES
PREPARATION TIME: 40 MINUTES

10 saffron threads
3 tablespoons white wine
8 wafer-thin slices of baguette
Light olive oil, for frying
1 leek, white and light green parts
    only, sliced into thin rings
1 shallot, finely chopped
½ fennel bulb, cored and sliced
1 garlic clove, finely chopped
2 medium waxy potatoes, peeled
    and cut into ¾-inch (2 cm) cubes
10 cherry tomatoes, halved
2 cups (500 ml) Vegetable Stock
    (page 232)
9 ounces (250 g) monkfish fillet,
    cut into pieces
3 flat-leaf parsley sprigs, leaves
    only, finely chopped
2 dill sprigs
Salt and pepper, to taste
1 recipe Rouille (page 237), for
    serving

Preheat the oven to 350°F (180°C). Line a baking sheet with parchment paper.

Soak the saffron in the white wine for 15 to 30 minutes to extract all the flavor and color.

Meanwhile, arrange the baguette slices on the baking sheet. Bake for 4 to 6 minutes, until golden brown and crispy. Let cool.

Heat 1 tablespoon of olive oil in a medium pot over medium heat and sweat the leek, shallot, and fennel for 2 minutes, until they start to soften. Add the garlic and cook for another minute. Add the potatoes and stir briefly before deglazing the pan with the saffron-infused white wine. Add the tomatoes, lower the heat, pour in the stock, and simmer for 10 minutes.

Add the monkfish and parsley. Chop 1 of the dill sprigs and sprinkle it over the stew. Cover and cook for 4 to 6 minutes, then check to see if the potatoes are tender by inserting the tip of a knife; if it slides in easily, the potatoes are done.

Garnish the stew with the remaining dill sprig and serve with croutons and rouille.

CALORIES   477 —— FAT 11 G —— SAT FAT 2 G —— CARBS 62 G
SUGARS 9 G —— PROTEIN 31 G —— SODIUM 459 MG —— FIBER 11 G

CHRAIME
with Eggplant, Fennel & Flounder

This is a recipe inspired by the book *TLV* by food writer Jigal Krant, who introduced me to the vivid flavors of the Israeli kitchen. You braise the vegetables for a very long time at a very low temperature, while adding a slew of seasonings. The fish is then gently cooked in the vegetable sauce.

SERVES 2
PREPARATION TIME: 1 HOUR AND 15 MINUTES

Light olive oil, for frying
2 bell peppers, seeded and cut into 1-inch (2.5 cm) pieces
½ eggplant, cut into ¾-inch (2 cm) cubes
1 fennel bulb, cored and coarsely chopped
1 red chile, sliced into rings
2 salted anchovy fillets, soaked to remove excess salt and drained
4 garlic cloves, coarsely chopped
2 teaspoons cumin seeds
1 teaspoon caraway seeds
1 teaspoon fennel seeds
1½ teaspoons smoked paprika
1 tablespoon tomato paste
One 14-ounce (400 g) can whole peeled tomatoes
1 bay leaf
Fish Stock (page 232; optional)
Salt, to taste
Juice of ¼ lemon
2 flounder fillets (3 to 4 ounces/100 g each)
3 cilantro sprigs, leaves only

TECHINA
2 tablespoons tahini
Juice of ½ lemon
1 garlic clove, finely chopped

Heat a splash of oil in a deep, heavy-bottomed frying pan over medium-low heat and sweat the bell peppers, eggplant, fennel, red chile, anchovies, and garlic until softened but not browned, 10 minutes.

Grind the cumin, caraway, and fennel seeds in a mortar. Mix in the paprika, followed by the tomato paste. Add to the pan. Crush the peeled tomatoes and their juices in a bowl with a masher and add them to the pan, too. Reduce the heat to low and add the bay leaf. Let the sauce simmer for 40 to 45 minutes to allow the flavors to blend. Add a spoonful of fish stock if the sauce thickens too much. Taste and season with salt and lemon juice.

Submerge the fillets in the sauce and cook the fish over low heat for 10 to 15 minutes, making sure the sauce remains at a gentle simmer. The fish is cooked properly when it can be easily pierced with the tip of a knife.

Meanwhile, make the techina by mixing the tahini, lemon juice, and garlic in a small bowl. The mixture will thicken slightly. Turn it into a smooth dressing by adding a few tablespoons of water in a slow trickle while whisking constantly.

Scatter the cilantro on top of the chraime and serve with the techina dressing.

CALORIES 451 — FAT 17 G — SAT FAT 3 G — CARBS 47 G
SUGARS 16 G — PROTEIN 31 G — SODIUM 743 MG — FIBER 14 G

VEGETABLE TAGINE
with Ras el Hanout & Halibut

My dear friend David Loftus, the photographer of this book, inspired me to learn more about Moroccan cuisine after his wedding in beautiful Marrakech, where I was privileged to be part of the wedding dinner. The simplicity, the ingredients, the elegance, the harmony of Moroccan recipes are just wonderful. This is my take on a tagine. It's delicious with couscous.

SERVES 2
PREPARATION TIME: 50 MINUTES

Light olive oil, for frying
2 medium yellow onions, sliced
    into thin rings
1 bell pepper, seeded and sliced
½ medium eggplant, cut into
    1-inch (2.5 cm) pieces
1 garlic clove, thinly sliced
8 flat-leaf parsley sprigs, leaves
    picked, stems coarsely chopped
1 teaspoon ras el hanout
1 tablespoon dried rose petals
    (optional)
Pinch of cayenne pepper
1 large tomato, coarsely chopped
3 to 4 ounces (100 g) waxy
    potatoes, peeled, cut into ¼-inch
    (6 mm) slices, rinsed and patted
    dry
1¾ cups (400 ml) Vegetable Stock
    (page 232)
Salt and pepper, to taste
One 7-ounce (200 g) halibut fillet,
    halved
½ Preserved Lemon (page 237),
    rind only, thinly sliced
1 tablespoon raisins
1 tablespoon coarsely chopped
    roasted and blanched hazelnuts

Place a clay tagine or a wide, shallow, heavy-bottomed frying pan over medium-high heat. Add a generous splash of olive oil, followed by the onions. Sweat them, stirring constantly, for 5 minutes, until they're soft and sweet but not browned.

Add the bell pepper, eggplant, and garlic and cook for 5 minutes more. Lower the heat, if needed, to stop the garlic from burning. Add the parsley stems and mix well. Push everything to one side of the pan and add the ras el hanout and the rose petals (if using) to the empty side. Fry until aromatic, 1 minute.

Add the cayenne pepper and stir to combine all the contents of the pan. Add the tomato and potatoes and stir. Pour in the vegetable stock. Cover the pan, lower the heat to low, and simmer for 10 to 12 minutes, until the potatoes are barely tender.

Uncover the pan and season with salt and pepper. Place the halibut, lemon rind, and raisins on top of the stew. Ladle over some of the sauce so the fish is just covered. Replace the lid and steam the fish until cooked through, 4 to 6 minutes. The fish is cooked properly when it can be easily pierced with the tip of a knife.

Check if the potatoes are tender by inserting the tip of a knife; if it slides in easily, the potatoes are done. Scatter the parsley leaves and hazelnuts on top and serve.

CALORIES 424 —— FAT 20 G —— SAT FAT 3 G —— CARBS 41 G
SUGARS 22 G —— PROTEIN 28 G —— SODIUM 483 MG —— FIBER 12 G

THAI GREEN CURRY
with Tiger Prawns

Red, green, or yellow Thai curry? The difference lies in the color of the chiles used for the curry pastes. Each has its own distinct flavor. The green and yellow varieties tend to be milder than the red and are therefore particularly good in vegetable dishes with fish.

SERVES 2
PREPARATION TIME: 30 MINUTES

1 cup (200 g) basmati or pandan
   rice
Salt and pepper, to taste
5 ounces (150 g) snow peas,
   strings removed
Light olive oil, for frying
8 large tiger prawns, heads
   removed, peeled, and deveined
½ red onion, coarsely chopped
2 tablespoons Green Curry Paste
   (page 234)
3 to 4 ounces (100 g) broccolini
½ head of bok choy, root end
   trimmed, coarsely chopped
Generous ¾ cup (200 ml) coconut
   milk
¼ cup (40 g) bean sprouts
1 tablespoon raw cashews,
   coarsely chopped
2 Thai basil sprigs, leaves only
½ lime, cut into wedges

Rinse the rice in a sieve under cold running water, drain, and transfer to a medium saucepan. Add enough water to cover the rice so it comes up to your second knuckle. Add a big pinch of salt and bring to a boil. Lower the heat, cover, and cook the rice until al dente, about 8 minutes. Remove from the heat, fluff with a fork, and keep warm with the lid on.

Fill a bowl with ice water. Bring a saucepan full of salted water to a boil and blanch the snow peas for 4 to 5 minutes, until bright green. Scoop them out of the pan with a skimmer and transfer them immediately to the ice water to cool. Drain, then pat dry with a kitchen towel.

Heat 1 tablespoon oil in a frying pan or wok over medium-high heat and fry the prawns until caramelized, 1 to 2 minutes on each side. Remove from the pan and set aside.

Heat another 1 tablespoon oil in the same pan over medium-high heat and sauté the onion for 1 to 2 minutes, until softened. Add the curry paste and cook until fragrant, 1 minute. Add the broccolini and bok choy and cook for 1 minute more. Pour in the coconut milk and add the snow peas. Turn the heat to low and let everything simmer, stirring occasionally, for 4 to 5 minutes, to allow the flavors to blend. Add the prawns and bean sprouts and stir.

Top the curry with the cashew nuts, Thai basil, and lime. Serve with the rice on the side.

CALORIES 810 —— FAT 40 G —— SAT FAT 14 G —— CARBS 93 G
SUGARS 13 G —— PROTEIN 24 G —— SODIUM 324 MG —— FIBER 8 G

BARBECUE

SEAWEED-SALMON BURGERS
WITH CELERY RÉMOULADE — 185

COLESLAW
WITH TZATZIKI & SPICY
SARDINES — 187

BABY ROMAINE
WITH TOMATOES & BARBECUED
TROUT — 188

ROASTED MUSHROOMS & PARSNIPS
WITH GRILLED OCTOPUS — 191

VEGETABLE SKEWERS
WITH PRAWNS & RAVIGOTE
SAUCE — 192

GADO-GADO
WITH SATE LILIT — 196

The chemical reaction between carbohydrates and amino acids in the presence of heat is known as the Maillard reaction. This is what gives us the nice brown color, but more importantly, the great flavor and texture we associate with baked bread and grilled meat and fish. The higher the temperature, the greater the reaction. That's why grilled food has that unique flavor we all love so much. This chapter features a few gorgeous veggie-and-fish dishes to make on the barbecue. And if you don't have a barbecue, a cast-iron grill pan will do (almost) as good a job.

SEAWEED-SALMON BURGERS
with Celery Rémoulade

Since entering the world of fish, I have taken inspiration not just from fish and shellfish, but also from the many different seaweeds that are found in the ocean. Seaweed is rich in iron, fiber, and protein, making it not only delicious, but also extremely healthy. When looking to buy kelp for this recipe, seek out locally sourced options (see page 13).

SERVES 2
PREPARATION TIME: 1 HOUR

½ ounce (15 g) dried kelp or wakame
1½ tablespoons butter
1 leek, white and light green parts only, sliced into thin rings
Salt and pepper, to taste
Scant ¼ cup (30 g) canned chickpeas, rinsed and drained
1 tablespoon Green Curry Paste (page 234)
3 to 4 ounces (100 g) skinless salmon fillet, cut into small pieces
½ shallot, very finely chopped
1 egg
1 tablespoon panko (Japanese bread crumbs)
⅔ cup (150 ml) white wine vinegar
1 teaspoon sugar
1 red onion, sliced into rings
Oil, for brushing
2 hamburger buns, split
4 leaves of iceberg lettuce

CELERY RÉMOULADE
1 celery stalk, finely diced
1 gherkin, finely chopped
1 shallot, finely chopped
¼ cup (60 ml) Mayonnaise (page 236)
A few drops of hot sauce
A few drops of fresh lemon juice

Place the seaweed in a bowl with 2 cups (500 ml) of hot water and let it rehydrate for 10 minutes. Drain in a colander for 5 minutes and leave to cool. Squeeze out any remaining liquid with your hands before cutting it into ¼-inch (6 mm) pieces. Set aside.

Meanwhile, melt the butter in a frying pan over medium-high heat. Add the leek and stir well before adding 1 tablespoon of water. Cover and braise the leek until soft, 10 minutes. Remove the lid and, stirring constantly, let the water evaporate. Season with salt and pepper and set aside.

Grind the chickpeas in a food processor. Transfer to a bowl and mix in the curry paste. Add the salmon, shallot, egg, and seaweed, and work it all together with your hands. Add the panko and a pinch of salt, if you like, and mix to combine. Shape the mixture into two patties. Cover and chill in the fridge for 20 to 30 minutes.

Light the barbecue.

Bring the vinegar and ⅔ cup (150 ml) water to a boil in a small saucepan. Add 1 teaspoon salt and the sugar and stir until the sugar dissolves. Place the onion rings in a small bowl and pour over the brine. Marinate for 10 minutes, then drain.

Meanwhile, make the rémoulade. Fill a bowl with ice water. Bring a small saucepan of water to a boil. Blanch the celery for 1 to 2 minutes, until softened. Scoop it out of the pan with a skimmer and transfer immediately to the ice water to cool. Drain, then pat dry with a kitchen towel. Mix the celery with the gherkin, shallot, and mayonnaise in a small bowl. Season with hot sauce, lemon juice, salt, and pepper.

Brush both sides of the patties with oil and grill them until caramelized and cooked through, 3 to 4 minutes on each side. Briefly grill the buns, if you like. Spread the bottom bun with the rémoulade and build the burgers in the following order: iceberg lettuce, patty, leek, onion, and finally the top bun.

CALORIES 761 —— FAT 53 G —— SAT FAT 12 G —— CARBS 50 G
SUGARS 13 G —— PROTEIN 22 G —— SODIUM 901 MG —— FIBER 8 G

COLESLAW
with Tzatziki & Spicy Sardines

Tzatziki is a great dressing for firm vegetables like cabbage. But it's also a refreshing dip to serve with grilled fish. For a thick and luscious sauce, always use full-fat yogurt, and remember to drain the cucumber until all the liquid is removed.

SERVES 2
ADVANCE PREPARATION TIME:
30 MINUTES
PREPARATION TIME: 30 MINUTES

TZATZIKI
½ cucumber, peeled and seeded
Salt and pepper, to taste
2 garlic cloves, coarsely chopped
2 tablespoons light olive oil
1¾ cups (400 g) full-fat plain
   yogurt
Juice of ½ lemon
6 mint leaves, finely chopped
3 dill sprigs, leaves only, finely
   chopped

1 cup (60 g) thinly sliced red
   cabbage
1 cup (60 g) thinly sliced green
   cabbage
1 cup (60 g) thinly sliced napa
   cabbage
1 Granny Smith apple, cored and
   thinly sliced
2 mint sprigs, leaves only, coarsely
   chopped
1 tablespoon light olive oil
½ teaspoon ground chile
6 fresh sardines, cleaned

To make the tzatziki, grate the cucumber, sprinkle with salt, and leave to drain in a sieve, preferably overnight, to draw out most of the moisture. If you're pressed for time, wrap a kitchen towel around the cucumber after 30 minutes and squeeze out any remaining liquid.

Mash the garlic in a mortar or a food processor. Add the olive oil. Combine the yogurt, cucumber, and garlic oil in a small bowl. Season with the lemon juice, mint, dill, salt, and pepper.

Light the barbecue.

Combine the red, green, and napa cabbages with the apple and mint in a medium bowl.

Mix the oil with the ground chile in a small bowl and lightly brush the sardines with it. Grill the sardines for 2 to 3 minutes on each side until they're golden brown.

Mix half of the tzatziki with the coleslaw and serve the other half with the sardines.

> **TIP:** To prevent the sardines from sticking to the grate, cover it with a sheet of aluminum foil or use a dedicated fish grilling basket.

CALORIES 697 —— FAT 39 G —— SAT FAT 8 G —— CARBS 30 G
SUGAR 21 G —— PROTEIN 59 G —— SODIUM 417 MG —— FIBER 4 G

BABY ROMAINE
with Tomatoes & Barbecued Trout

We usually eat lettuce raw, dressed with some oil and vinegar or a dairy-based dressing. But like so many other vegetables, lettuce can also be grilled on the barbecue. I brush it with a marinade instead of a dressing.

SERVES 2
PREPARATION TIME: 30 MINUTES

MARINADE
1 teaspoon red pepper flakes
1 teaspoon coriander seeds
1 teaspoon cumin seeds
½ teaspoon mustard seeds
Salt, to taste
3 garlic cloves, coarsely chopped
4 oregano sprigs, leaves only
Juice of 1 lemon
¾ cup (150 ml) light olive oil

4 baby romaine hearts, halved
   lengthwise
2 cups (250 g) cherry tomatoes,
   halved
2 trout (7 ounces/200 g each),
   cleaned
Flaky salt (like Maldon or fleur de
   sel), for serving
Extra virgin olive oil, for serving
   (optional)

Light the barbecue.

To make the marinade, grind the red pepper flakes, coriander, cumin, and mustard seeds with a pinch of salt in a mortar or food processor. Add the garlic and oregano and mash to form a smooth paste. Mix in the lemon juice and olive oil. Season with salt.

Brush the marinade onto the cut sides of the romaine and tomatoes as well as both sides of the fish. If you have one, place the trout in a fish grilling basket to prevent it from sticking to the grate.

Grill the trout until the skin is crispy, 3 to 4 minutes on each side. When you flip the trout, place the lettuce and tomatoes on the grate. Grill them for 3 to 4 minutes, until lightly browned.

Transfer the lettuce and tomatoes to plates and top with the fish. Serve with a sprinkle of flaky salt and a splash of olive oil (if you like).

CALORIES 619 —— FAT 50 G —— SAT FAT 8 G —— CARBS 14 G
SUGARS 5 G —— PROTEIN 31 G —— SODIUM 164 MG —— FIBER 6 G

ROASTED MUSHROOMS & PARSNIPS
with Grilled Octopus

In this recipe, octopus is braised before it's briefly grilled over high heat. This results in lightly caramelized tentacles with a delicious but subtle barbecue flavor. It's great with a classic olive mayonnaise.

SERVES 2
PREPARATION TIME: 40 MINUTES

1 medium parsnip, cut into ½-inch (13 mm) batons
2 portobello mushrooms, coarsely chopped
Extra virgin olive oil
Salt and pepper, to taste
10 cherry tomatoes, halved

OLIVE MAYONNAISE
Generous ¾ cup (200 ml) Mayonnaise (page 236)
20 kalamata olives, pitted
1 oil-packed anchovy fillet, drained
Juice of ½ lime

10 to 11 ounces (300 g) octopus tentacles, cooked (see page 78)
Flaky salt (like Maldon or fleur de sel)

Preheat the oven to 400°F (200°C). Light the barbecue.

Line a baking pan with parchment paper and arrange the parsnip and mushrooms on it. Drizzle with olive oil and sprinkle with salt. Roast the vegetables for 25 minutes total, until nicely charred. Add the tomatoes, cut sides up, after 20 minutes.

Meanwhile, make the olive mayonnaise by blending the mayonnaise, olives, and anchovy in a blender or with an immersion blender. Season with lime juice, salt, and pepper.

Brush the octopus tentacles with oil and grill them for 3 to 4 minutes, until they start to caramelize on the outside.

Serve the roasted vegetables with the octopus, mayonnaise, flaky salt, and freshly ground pepper.

CALORIES 639 —— FAT 49 G —— SAT FAT 7 G —— CARBS 27 G
SUGARS 8 G —— PROTEIN 26 G —— SODIUM 709 MG —— FIBER 7 G

VEGETABLE SKEWERS
with Prawns & Ravigote Sauce

There are many variations of ravigote to be found, often made with mayonnaise. But the classic French version is a vinaigrette made with oil and vinegar and seasoned with fresh herbs. A finely chopped hard-boiled egg binds it all together. You'll need 6 skewers; if you use bamboo skewers, soak them in water while you prepare everything else, to prevent them from burning.

SERVES 2
PREPARATION TIME: 30 MINUTES

RAVIGOTE SAUCE

1 egg
2 teaspoons Dijon mustard
3 tablespoons white wine vinegar
¾ cup (150 ml) extra virgin olive oil
2 teaspoons capers, rinsed, drained, and finely chopped
3 chervil sprigs, leaves only, finely chopped
4 chives, finely chopped
4 flat-leaf parsley sprigs, leaves only, finely chopped
4 tarragon sprigs, leaves only, finely chopped
Salt and pepper, to taste

6 large head-on prawns or shrimp
½ medium zucchini, cut into large chunks
½ medium eggplant, cut into large chunks
½ bell pepper, seeded and cut into large chunks
Light olive oil, for brushing
20 green asparagus spears, woody ends removed, 1¼ inch (3 cm) cut off the ends
6 small yellow onions, halved

Light the barbecue.

To make the ravigote sauce, bring enough water to cover the egg to a boil in a small pot. Add the egg and cook for about 8 minutes, until hard-boiled. Cool under cold running water, then peel.

Whisk the mustard and vinegar together in a small bowl, then whisk in the olive oil. Add the capers, chervil, chives, parsley, and tarragon. Using the back of a spoon or a spatula, press the hard-boiled egg through a sieve into the vinaigrette. Season with salt and pepper.

Thread 1 prawn onto a skewer, followed by a few chunks of zucchini, eggplant, and bell pepper. Repeat this for all the skewers. Brush with oil and sprinkle with salt and pepper. Lightly brush the asparagus and onions with oil.

Place the skewers, asparagus, and onions on the grate and grill until charred, 5 to 6 minutes, flipping halfway through. Depending on their size, the onions may take a bit longer.

Serve the skewers with the asparagus and onions, and the ravigote sauce on the side.

CALORIES 441 —— FAT 29 G —— SAT FAT 4 G —— CARBS 36 G
SUGARS 22 G —— PROTEIN 15 G —— SODIUM 93 MG —— FIBER 11 G

GADO-GADO with Sate Lilit

Here is my take on sate lilit, the famous Balinese fish satay, which is delicious served with gado-gado—a beloved Indonesian vegetable-rich dish—and spicy homemade peanut sauce. You can use any kind of white fish for this recipe, or even white fish trimmings for a more affordable option. Sambal badjak is an Indonesian chile condiment, found in Asian grocery stores.

SERVES 2
PREPARATION TIME: 50 MINUTES

SATE LILIT

7 ounces (200 g) skinless, boneless white fish
3 to 4 ounces (100 g) tiger prawns, heads removed, peeled, and deveined
¾-inch (2 cm) piece of turmeric, minced, or 1 teaspoon ground turmeric
2 makrut lime leaves, julienned
2½ tablespoons coconut milk
1 tablespoon sugar
Salt and pepper, to taste
6 lemongrass stalks
Oil, for brushing
2 tablespoons unsalted peanuts, finely chopped

GADO-GADO

5 ounces (145 g) green beans, trimmed
12 green asparagus tips
½ cucumber, seeded
¼ head of napa cabbage
2 medium carrots, peeled
¼ cup (30 g) bean sprouts
2 eggs

PEANUT SAUCE

¾-inch (2 cm) piece of ginger, peeled and coarsely chopped
1 garlic clove, coarsely chopped
1 tablespoon unsalted peanuts
1 sheet of nori, torn into large pieces
Oil, for frying
1 generous cup (250 ml) coconut milk
Heaping ⅓ cup (100 g) creamy natural peanut butter
1 tablespoon brown sugar
2 teaspoons sambal badjak
Juice of ½ lime

To prepare the sate, finely chop the fish and prawns. Mix the fish, prawns, turmeric, lime leaves, coconut milk, and sugar in a bowl. Season with salt and pepper. Divide the mixture into 6 equal portions and mold around the lemongrass stalks with your hands. Place them in the fridge on a plate to firm up for at least 30 minutes.

To make the gado-gado, bring a generous amount of water with a pinch of salt to a boil in a saucepan. Cook the beans until just tender, 4 to 6 minutes total. Add the asparagus tips after about 3 minutes and cook until tender-crisp. Drain the vegetables, then run them under cold water to stop the cooking process. Pat dry with a kitchen towel.

While the vegetables cook, slice the cucumber, cabbage, and carrots into long strips.

Bring enough water to cover the eggs to a boil in a small pot. Add the eggs and boil for 6 minutes. (The eggs will be medium boiled, with the yolks just set.) Cool the eggs under cold running water, then peel and halve them lengthwise. Set aside.

Light the barbecue.

To make the peanut sauce, process the ginger, garlic, peanuts, and nori in a food processor until finely ground. Heat the oil in a pan over medium heat and fry the mixture for 1 minute, until fragrant. Stir in the coconut milk, peanut butter, brown sugar, and sambal badjak. Let the sauce simmer gently until you're ready to serve. Add the lime juice just before serving.

Brush the sate with oil and grill for 4 to 6 minutes, turning occasionally so they're evenly browned and cooked through on all sides.

Arrange the vegetables, eggs, and sates on a platter. Pour the peanut sauce over everything and sprinkle with the peanuts.

CALORIES 608 —— FAT 35 G —— SAT FAT 9 G —— CARBS 36 G
SUGARS 19 G —— PROTEIN 40 G —— SODIUM 226 MG —— FIBER 9 G

OVEN

SOLE EN PAPILLOTE
WITH HARISSA — 201

ROASTED VEGETABLES
WITH BURRATA & SARDINES — 202

MISO EGGPLANT
WITH FRIED MACKEREL — 204

VEGETABLE GRATIN "ROGER VERGÉ"
WITH ANCHOVIES — 207

SWEET POTATO QUICHE
WITH COD CHEEKS — 208

ROASTED CARROTS & TURBOT
WITH GREMOLATA — 210

ROASTED VEGETABLES
WITH WHOLE SEA BASS — 213

RICE SALAD
WITH HERB-CRUSTED MULLET — 214

LEEKS & FENNEL
WITH SARDINES & MINT
PESTO — 217

After you've done all the prep in the kitchen, the oven does the rest, leaving you with time to spend on other things. Hardy vegetables cook especially well in the oven. A high temperature ensures tenderness and a pleasant hint of bitterness from the slight charring. When preparing vegetables and fish, take the sizes and cooking times into account. They have to be roughly equal for all ingredients.

SOLE EN PAPILLOTE
with Harissa

Cooking fish and vegetables in a parcel in the oven is easy and delicious. It keeps in all of the flavors and juices, and they combine to form a wonderful sauce. The harissa gives this dish a spicy kick. Any type of flatfish, such as flounder, would work well in this recipe.

SERVES 2
PREPARATION TIME: 50 MINUTES

1½ teaspoons red harissa
¼ cup (60 ml) Fish Stock (page 232)
1 sole (about 12 ounces/350 g), skin removed
1 beefsteak tomato, thinly sliced
1 red bell pepper, seeded and thinly sliced
1 small carrot, peeled and cut into thin rounds
½ red onion, sliced into thin rings
1 teaspoon cumin seeds
Salt, to taste
1 Preserved Lemon (page 237), rind only, thinly sliced
3 cilantro sprigs, leaves only

Preheat the oven to 350°F (180°C).

Cover a sheet of aluminum foil, about twice the size of the fish, with a sheet of parchment paper. Turn the edges up slightly to create a "boat" to keep the liquids from leaking.

Combine half of the harissa with the fish stock in a medium bowl. Lightly coat the sole on one side with the remaining harissa.

Mix the tomato, bell pepper, carrot, onion, and cumin seeds with the harissa–fish stock mixture.

Remove the tomatoes from the stock and place them in the middle of the parchment paper, overlapping slightly. Arrange the carrot, bell pepper, and onion on top of the tomatoes. Sprinkle with salt.

Place the sole on the vegetables, harissa side up. Top with the preserved lemon rind.

Close the parcel, leaving a small opening. Pour in the remaining stock mixture and close the parcel completely. Make sure there's enough room inside for the steam to circulate.

Place the parcel on a baking sheet and bake for 30 to 35 minutes, until the fish is cooked through and easily falls off the bone.

Carefully open the parcel at the table, and sprinkle with the cilantro.

CALORIES 140 —— FAT 2 G —— SAT FAT 0 G —— CARBS 20 G
SUGARS 9 G —— PROTEIN 15 G —— SODIUM 894 MG —— FIBER 6 G

ROASTED VEGETABLES
with Burrata & Sardines

Sardines can be prepared with the head on or off. To get the sardines to fry up crisply, don't use too much oil, and sprinkle them with a generous pinch of salt. This dish can also be made with buffalo mozzarella in place of the burrata.

SERVES 2
PREPARATION TIME: 45 MINUTES

Extra virgin olive oil
1 medium eggplant, cut into
  ¼-inch (6 mm) slices
1 medium zucchini, cut into ¼-inch
  (6 mm) slices
1 red bell pepper, seeded and
  coarsely chopped
1 yellow bell pepper, seeded and
  coarsely chopped
1 red onion, coarsely chopped
1 fennel bulb, cored and coarsely
  chopped
½ garlic bulb, halved crosswise
Salt and pepper, to taste
6 fresh sardines, cleaned, with or
  without heads
Oil, for frying
3 marjoram sprigs, leaves only
1 burrata (about 4½ ounces/125 g)

Preheat the oven to 350°F (180°C).

Line a rimmed baking sheet with parchment paper and drizzle with olive oil. Arrange the eggplant, zucchini, bell pepper, onion, and fennel on the baking sheet and place the garlic in the center. Drizzle with more olive oil and sprinkle with salt and pepper. Roast the vegetables for about 25 minutes, until golden brown.

Pat the sardines dry with a paper towel and sprinkle with salt on both sides. Heat a little oil in a frying pan over medium heat. Fry the sardines until golden brown on both sides, 3 to 5 minutes, flipping halfway. Remove the sardines from the pan and set aside on paper towels to drain.

Toss the roasted vegetables with a generous splash of olive oil and the marjoram, and season with salt and pepper. Arrange the vegetables on an ovenproof platter. Separate the garlic into individual cloves and scatter them over the vegetables. Break the burrata into large pieces and scatter them over the roasted vegetables. Put the platter into the oven for about 2 minutes, until the cheese is warmed through.

Arrange the sardines on top of the vegetables and sprinkle with freshly ground pepper.

CALORIES 723 —— FAT 39 G —— SAT FAT 12 G —— CARBS 37 G
SUGARS 15 G —— PROTEIN 63 G —— SODIUM 466 MG —— FIBER 13 G

MISO EGGPLANT
with Fried Mackerel

A Japanese-inspired miso sauce gives this dish its utterly delicious umami flavor. Both the mackerel and the vegetables are brushed with the sauce. The soft and meaty roasted eggplant pairs well with deep-fried slices of ginger and garlic, which provide lots of crunch.

SERVES 2
PREPARATION TIME: 40 MINUTES

2 eggplants, halved lengthwise
2 tablespoons raw sesame oil
1 tablespoon white sesame seeds
2 tablespoons mirin
2 tablespoons sake
2 tablespoons sugar
2 tablespoons white miso
Oil, for frying
2-inch (5 cm) piece of ginger,
  thinly sliced
1 garlic clove, thinly sliced
1 scallion, thinly sliced
2 skin-on mackerel fillets (about
  3 ounces/90 g each)

Preheat the oven to 400°F (200°C). Line a baking sheet with parchment paper.

Cut a diamond pattern in the cut surfaces of the eggplant halves by scoring them diagonally in both directions at ½-inch (13 mm) intervals. Brush with the sesame oil. Place the eggplant on the baking sheet, cut side down. Bake the eggplant for about 20 minutes, until tender. Remove from the oven.

Meanwhile, heat a small frying pan over medium heat and toast the sesame seeds until golden brown. Transfer to a plate and set aside.

Heat the mirin, sake, and sugar in a small saucepan. Turn off the heat when the sugar has dissolved. Whisk in the miso.

In a small, heavy-bottomed saucepan, heat a ½-inch (13 mm) layer of oil to 350°F (180°C). Deep-fry the ginger and garlic until crisp, 1 to 2 minutes. Do not let the garlic get too dark, or it will be bitter. Remove from the oil with a slotted spoon and drain immediately on paper towels.

Turn on the broiler.

Brush the cut sides of the eggplant with 2 tablespoons of the miso sauce. Place the eggplant under the broiler for a few minutes, until slightly caramelized. Remove from the oven, then cut the eggplant into chunks and mix with the scallion.

Heat 1 tablespoon oil in a large frying pan over medium heat and fry the mackerel fillets, skin side down, for 2 to 3 minutes, until caramelized. Flip, then cook for 1 minute on the other side, until crispy on the outside and soft on the inside.

Sprinkle the sesame seeds over the eggplant-scallion mixture, and drizzle with a tablespoon of miso sauce. Top with the deep-fried ginger and garlic. Serve with the mackerel fillets and the rest of the sauce.

CALORIES 573 —— FAT 29 G —— SAT FAT 4 G —— CARBS 60 G
SUGARS 36 G —— PROTEIN 25 G —— SODIUM 962 MG —— FIBER 16 G

VEGETABLE GRATIN "ROGER VERGÉ"
with Anchovies

At the tender age of ten, I was already fascinated by top-level gastronomy. We used to go to France on vacation, and when we did our daily shopping, we'd pass the three-star restaurant of legendary French chef Roger Vergé. From between the cypress trees, I'd peer inside. Vergé was known for his vegetable dishes, including this gratin. This is my humble ode to the great master, with the addition of anchovies, cheese, and walnuts.

SERVES 2
PREPARATION TIME: 50 MINUTES

2 tablespoons light olive oil
2 medium yellow onions, sliced into rings
Salt and pepper, to taste
1 garlic clove, peeled
5 large tomatoes (14 ounces/ 400 g), cut into ¼-inch (6 mm) slices
1 zucchini, cut into ¼-inch (6 mm) rounds
1 tablespoon fresh thyme leaves, plus extra for garnish
4 tablespoons (60 ml) extra virgin olive oil
8 oil-packed anchovy fillets, drained
¼ cup (30 g) freshly grated Comté
6 whole walnuts, coarsely chopped

Preheat the oven to 400°F (200°C).

Heat the light olive oil in a frying pan over medium heat. Fry the onions until soft, around 10 minutes; they shouldn't brown. Season with salt and pepper.

Rub the inside of an 8-inch (20 cm) round baking dish with the garlic clove, then discard the garlic. Arrange the onions on the bottom of the dish. Top with alternating and overlapping slices of tomato and zucchini. Sprinkle with the thyme leaves and drizzle with 2 tablespoons of the extra virgin olive oil.

Bake the vegetables for 25 minutes, until nicely browned. Arrange the anchovies on top of the vegetables and sprinkle the cheese over everything. Return to the oven for 5 minutes more, until the cheese and anchovies are melted.

Remove from the oven and drizzle over the remaining 2 tablespoons extra virgin olive oil. Top with the walnuts and thyme.

CALORIES 652 — FAT 55 G — SAT FAT 10 G — CARBS 35 G
SUGARS 21 G — PROTEIN 16 G — SODIUM 660 MG — FIBER 9 G

SWEET POTATO QUICHE
with Cod Cheeks

Cod cheeks have become a somewhat overlooked part of the fish. They have a distinctive, firm texture. They used to be made into batter-fried kibbeling, one of my favorite Dutch street foods. And they can also be used for fish and chips. But there are so many more possibilities! If you can't find cod cheeks, regular cod fillets work well for this recipe.

SERVES 4
PREPARATION TIME: 1 HOUR AND 20 MINUTES

1 tablespoon butter
One 14-ounce (400 g) sheet of puff pastry, thawed if frozen
1 pound (500 g) sweet potatoes
4 green asparagus spears, woody ends removed
Light olive oil, for frying
7 ounces (200 g) button mushrooms, halved
2 tablespoons dry sherry
1 shallot, finely chopped
2 leeks, white part only, sliced into thin rings
10 to 11 ounces (300 g) cod cheeks
Salt and pepper, to taste
4 eggs, beaten
½ cup (125 ml) light cream

Preheat the oven to 400°F (200°C).

Grease an 8-inch (20 cm) springform pan with butter. Ease the puff pastry into the pan and gently press it down into the pan with your hands.

To blind-bake the crust, place a sheet of parchment paper over the puff pastry, cover with pie weights or dried beans, and bake for 10 minutes, until barely golden. Remove the parchment paper and weights and bake the crust for another 5 minutes, until lightly baked. Remove the crust from the oven and lower the temperature to 350°F (180°C).

Meanwhile, bring a large pot of water to a boil and cook the sweet potatoes until fork-tender, about 16 to 20 minutes. Drain, peel, and cut into ¼-inch (6 mm) slices.

Fill a bowl with ice water. Bring a saucepan of water to a boil. Blanch the asparagus for 2 minutes, until bright green. Scoop them out of the pan with a skimmer and transfer to the ice water to stop the cooking process. Drain, pat dry with a kitchen towel, then cut the asparagus in half lengthwise.

Heat a splash of olive oil in a large frying pan over medium heat and fry the mushrooms until golden brown, 4 to 6 minutes. Deglaze with the sherry. Add the shallot and leeks, cover, and cook for 5 minutes, until softened. Transfer the vegetables to a large bowl. Wipe out the frying pan and return it to the heat.

Sprinkle the cod cheeks with salt. Heat a little olive oil in the frying pan over medium-high heat and fry the cod cheeks for 2 minutes on each side, until golden brown. Transfer to a plate and let cool.

Add the sweet potato, cod cheeks, eggs, and cream to the vegetables. Season with salt and pepper and gently mix. Pour into the pastry crust and top with the asparagus.

Bake the quiche for 30 to 35 minutes, until the top is nicely browned. Serve warm.

CALORIES 811 — FAT 51 G — SAT FAT 28 G — CARBS 60 G
SUGAR 14 G — PROTEIN 27 G — SODIUM 607 MG — FIBER 3 G

ROASTED CARROTS & TURBOT
with Gremolata

Carrots and fish are a perfect match, a classic and time-honored combination. There are so many wonderful varieties of carrots available—orange, yellow, white, red, and purple—and roasting them intensifies their flavor. The flavor of the roasted vegetables pairs well with the fresh, smooth gremolata.

SERVES 2
PREPARATION TIME: 45 MINUTES

10 carrots, a mix of varieties and colors (21 ounces/600 g total), peeled, large ones halved lengthwise
2 rosemary sprigs
1 thyme sprig
Extra virgin olive oil
Salt and pepper, to taste
1 tablespoon balsamic vinegar

GREMOLATA
1 garlic clove, coarsely chopped
½ bunch of flat-leaf parsley, leaves only
Juice of ½ lemon
3 tablespoons extra virgin olive oil

7 ounces (200 g) skinless turbot fillet

Preheat the oven to 400°F (200°C).

Arrange the carrots, rosemary, and thyme in a deep baking dish. Drizzle with 3 tablespoons olive oil, mix, and season with salt and pepper. Bake for 20 to 30 minutes, turning the carrots halfway through. Remove from the oven as soon as the carrots can be easily pierced with the tip of a sharp knife. Mix in the balsamic vinegar. Set aside to keep warm.

Meanwhile, make the gremolata. Crush the garlic in a mortar with about ½ teaspoon salt. Add the parsley and continue grinding until the mixture is fairly smooth. Stir in the lemon juice and olive oil. Season with pepper.

Place a grill pan over high heat. Lightly brush the turbot with oil and season with salt. Grill the fish for 3 to 4 minutes on one side, until crispy on the outside and tender on the inside. Remove from the pan, cover with a piece of aluminum foil, and let sit for 4 to 5 minutes, until the fish is cooked through.

Serve the fish over the roasted carrots, with the gremolata on the side.

CALORIES 666 —— FAT 55 G —— SAT FAT 6 G —— CARBS 34 G
SUGARS 22 G —— PROTEIN 17 G —— SODIUM 808 MG —— FIBER 10 G

ROASTED VEGETABLES
with Whole Sea Bass

There's nothing more festive than a whole fish from the oven. Stuff the belly with your favorite aromatics, tuck vegetables around the fish, and bake everything together.

SERVES 2
PREPARATION TIME: 30 MINUTES

1 sea bass (17 to 21 ounces/500 to 600 g), cleaned
½ bunch of chervil, coarsely chopped
½ bunch of flat-leaf parsley, coarsely chopped
1 lemon, sliced
Zest of 1 orange, chopped
Extra virgin olive oil
Salt and pepper, to taste
2 bell peppers, seeded and sliced into rings
1 red onion, quartered
1 fennel bulb, cored and coarsely chopped
1 garlic bulb, halved crosswise
4 green asparagus spears, woody ends removed, halved lengthwise

Preheat the oven to 400°F (200°C).

Score the skin of the sea bass every inch (2.5 cm) so that the flesh is visible.

Fill the abdominal cavity of the fish with the chervil, parsley, half of the lemon slices, and the orange zest. Brush the fish with olive oil and sprinkle with salt.

Place the sea bass in a baking dish, and arrange the bell peppers, onion, fennel, garlic, asparagus, and the rest of the lemon slices around it. Bake for 18 to 20 minutes, until the vegetables and fish are cooked through. To test whether the fish is done, press the flesh away from the bone just behind the head. It should come away easily.

Serve drizzled with more olive oil, salt, and freshly ground pepper.

CALORIES 355 —— FAT 12 G —— SAT FAT 2 G —— CARBS 23 G
SUGARS 6 G —— PROTEIN 41 G —— SODIUM 209 MG —— FIBER 7 G

RICE SALAD
with Herb-Crusted Mullet

I coat these mullet fillets with a crumble made from panko and fresh herbs and spices. The crunchy golden-brown crust contrasts wonderfully with the tenderness of the fish.

SERVES 2
PREPARATION TIME: 1 HOUR

SALAD
⅔ cup (120 g) wild rice
1 medium carrot, peeled and cut into ¼-inch (6 mm) cubes
1 celery stalk, cut into ¼-inch (6 mm) cubes
1 scallion, thinly sliced
2 cilantro sprigs, leaves only

GINGER DRESSING
1 garlic clove, minced
¾-inch (2 cm) piece of ginger, peeled and grated
3 tablespoons raw sesame oil
1 tablespoon rice vinegar
1 tablespoon soy sauce
1 teaspoon honey

HERB CRUST
1 tablespoon butter
1 tablespoon raw sesame oil
1 garlic clove, finely minced
1 lemongrass stalk, white part only, thinly sliced crosswise
1 scallion, thinly sliced
½ red chile, seeded and finely minced
¾-inch (2 cm) piece of ginger, peeled and finely minced
4 cilantro sprigs, leaves only, finely chopped
1 tablespoon unsalted cashews, coarsely chopped
Zest of 1 lime
2 tablespoons panko (Japanese bread crumbs)
Salt and pepper, to taste

2 skinless mullet fillets (about 4 ounces/120 g each)

Bring a medium saucepan of water to a boil, add the wild rice, and cook until al dente, 40 to 50 minutes. Drain and set aside in a large bowl to cool.

Preheat the oven to 350°F (180°C).

To make the dressing, whisk together the garlic, ginger, sesame oil, vinegar, soy sauce, and honey in a small bowl. Set aside.

To make the herb crust, melt the butter in a saucepan over medium heat. Stir in the sesame oil, followed by the garlic, lemongrass, scallion, chile, and ginger. Stir for 1 minute, until fragrant. Add the cilantro, cashews, and lime zest, and season with salt. Remove from the heat. Stir in the panko; the mixture will be thick.

Place the mullet fillets in an oiled baking dish and cover with the herb-panko mixture. Bake for 7 to 9 minutes, until the crust is golden brown and the fish is flaky and opaque.

While the fish cooks, mix the carrot, celery, and scallion into the cooled wild rice. Stir in the dressing. Spoon the salad into a serving dish. Garnish with the cilantro.

Serve the mullet fillets on top of the salad or on the side.

CALORIES 700 —— FAT 36 G —— SAT FAT 6 G —— CARBS 64 G
SUGARS 13 G —— PROTEIN 35 G —— SODIUM 628 MG —— FIBER 6 G

LEEKS & FENNEL
with Sardines & Mint Pesto

The variations are endless when it comes to pesto, and it can be easily adapted to suit your personal tastes. You can use all kinds of nuts, as well as herbs other than basil. This pesto is made with mint, which adds a touch of freshness to the leeks and fennel.

SERVES 2
PREPARATION TIME: 40 MINUTES

3 leeks, white and light green parts only, halved lengthwise
5 green asparagus spears, woody ends removed
1 fennel bulb, cored and sliced
Extra virgin olive oil

MINT PESTO
1 garlic clove, coarsely chopped
6 mint sprigs, leaves only
Salt and pepper, to taste
¼ cup (30 g) pine nuts
⅓ cup (30 g) grated Parmesan
Scant ⅓ cup (75 ml) extra virgin olive oil

8 fresh sardines, cleaned, with or without heads
10 to 12 caperberries, rinsed and drained
1 mint sprig, leaves only, finely chopped

Preheat the oven to 400°F (200°C).

In a baking dish, toss the leeks, asparagus, and fennel with 2 tablespoons olive oil. Bake the vegetables for 12 to 15 minutes, until lightly caramelized and softened.

Meanwhile, make the pesto. In a mortar, grind the garlic with the mint and a pinch of salt. Add the pine nuts and continue grinding until finely crushed. Using a spoon, stir in the Parmesan, followed by the olive oil. You can also use an immersion blender to make the pesto, if you prefer. Set aside.

Remove the baking dish from the oven and arrange the sardines on top of the vegetables. Return the baking dish to the oven for another 7 to 10 minutes, until the fish is lightly colored and the flesh easily falls away from the bone. Add the caperberries after the sardines have cooked for about 5 minutes.

Drizzle with mint pesto and scatter over the mint leaves. Serve the rest of the mint pesto on the side.

CALORIES 797 —— FAT 45 G —— SAT FAT 6 G —— CARBS 30 G
SUGARS 7 G —— PROTEIN 74 G —— SODIUM 726 MG —— FIBER 7 G

PAN

Dishes that are cooked in a pan on the stovetop can be found throughout this book, but this section is all about recipes in which the pan really determines the flavor of the dish, whether it be pan-frying a fish to perfection, making a beautifully tender ratatouille or a classic hollandaise sauce, or my take on vegetables à la grecque. And this book wouldn't be complete without the inclusion of a Dutch mashed potato dish, an important part of my heritage.

RATATOUILLE
with Pan-Fried Cod & Fennel Gravy

In the 1990s, I worked as a cook at the restaurant Lucas Carton in Paris. It was there that I learned to prepare ratatouille at three-Michelin-star level, which involves cooking the vegetables individually before combining them.

SERVES 2
PREPARATION TIME: 45 MINUTES

2 large tomatoes
Extra virgin olive oil
2 bell peppers (whichever color you prefer), seeded, cut into ¼-inch (6 mm) cubes
½ medium eggplant, cut into ¼-inch (6 mm) cubes
½ medium zucchini, cut into ¼-inch (6 mm) cubes
2 thyme sprigs, plus extra for garnish
Salt and pepper, to taste

FENNEL GRAVY

1 medium fennel bulb, cored and sliced
1½ tablespoons dry vermouth or white wine
1 cup (240 ml) Fish Stock (page 232)
Scant ½ cup (100 ml) light cream

2 skin-on cod fillets (about 4 to 5 ounces/120 to 130 g each)

Bring enough water to just cover the tomatoes to a boil in a saucepan. Cut a shallow X into the bottom of each tomato. Submerge them in the boiling water for 10 to 20 seconds, then immediately remove with a skimmer and cool them under cold running water. Remove the skins, cut the tomatoes in half, and remove the seeds. Cut the flesh into small cubes.

Heat a splash of light olive oil in a frying pan or a saucepan over medium-high heat and cook the bell pepper until it softens, 3 to 4 minutes. Transfer to a plate. In the same frying pan, heat another splash of oil and cook the eggplant until it softens, 2 to 3 minutes. Transfer the eggplant to another plate. Add another splash of oil to the frying pan and cook the zucchini until soft, 2 to 3 minutes, then set it aside. All the ratatouille vegetables should be equally tender.

Combine the pepper, eggplant, and zucchini in a large saucepan. Add the thyme and tomatoes, pour in 3 tablespoons olive oil, and season with salt and pepper. Mix well and gently simmer, covered, over low heat for 10 minutes, to allow the flavors to blend. Turn the heat down as low as possible to keep the ratatouille warm.

Meanwhile, heat 1 tablespoon olive oil in a medium saucepan over medium-high heat and fry the fennel until softened, 4 to 6 minutes. Deglaze the pan with the vermouth, then add the fish stock and cream. Lower the heat and reduce the sauce by two-thirds, 7 to 10 minutes. Discard the fennel. Season with salt and pepper and set aside.

Pat the cod dry with a paper towel and sprinkle both sides with salt. Heat 2 tablespoons olive oil in a medium frying pan over medium-high heat and add the fish, skin side down. After 2 to 3 minutes, when the skin is crispy, carefully flip the fillets with a spatula. Fry the other side until the flesh is opaque, 1 to 2 minutes. Remove the fish from the pan.

Serve the ratatouille topped with the fish, skin side up, and a generous splash of olive oil. Serve the fennel sauce on the side.

CALORIES 775 — FAT 62 G — SAT FAT 15 G — CARBS 28 G
SUGARS 13 G — 32 G — SODIUM 186 MG — FIBER 9 G

ASPARAGUS & MARSH SAMPHIRE
with Hot-Smoked Salmon & Hollandaise Sauce

As soon as white asparagus is back in season, I rush to my local farmers' market. It's such a treat! I like to serve it the classic way with the king of sauces: sauce hollandaise. To reduce the risk of curdling, always make hollandaise with at least three egg yolks.

SERVES 2
PREPARATION TIME: 45 MINUTES

10 fat white asparagus spears, woody ends removed
⅔ cup (140 g) clarified butter, melted (see Note)
2½ cups (100 g) marsh samphire

HOLLANDAISE SAUCE
3 egg yolks
3 tablespoons white wine vinegar
Fresh lemon juice
Salt and pepper, to taste

5 to 6 ounces (150 g) skinned hot-smoked salmon, broken into large pieces and brought up to room temperature

NOTE: To make 1 cup (250 g) clarified butter: Slowly melt 1¼ cups (300 g) butter in a saucepan over low heat, making sure it doesn't brown. Remove the pan from the heat and skim the foam off the top with a spoon. Carefully pour the butterfat into a second pan, leaving the milky solids at the bottom of the saucepan.

Cut ¾ inch (2 cm) off the bottom of the asparagus spears and place the ends in a saucepan. Double-peel the asparagus by dragging a vegetable peeler from top to bottom, all the way around, then repeating the process. Add the peels to the pan with the ends. Add 4 cups (1 L) of water and bring to a boil.

Place the asparagus spears in a saucepan big enough for them to lie side by side without overlapping. Pour the boiling water and trimmings over the asparagus. Add a pinch of salt and cover with a kitchen towel to keep the asparagus submerged, making sure the towel is completely tucked inside the pan and doesn't hang over the sides. Bring to a boil and cook for 4 minutes. Turn off the heat and leave the asparagus in the pan, under the towel, for another 10 minutes, to finish cooking. The asparagus is done when you can slip the tip of a knife into the bottom with ease. Drain the asparagus spears (discard the ends and peelings) and pat dry with a clean towel. Keep warm.

Heat 1 tablespoon of the clarified butter in a frying pan over medium-high heat. Stir-fry the marsh samphire until soft, 2 minutes. Set aside.

To make the hollandaise sauce, prepare a bain marie: Bring a saucepan of water to a boil. Place a stainless-steel bowl on top of the saucepan, making sure it doesn't come into contact with the water. (You want the steam to warm the contents of the bowl, but not heat the sauce to boiling or it will separate.) Place the egg yolks and the vinegar in the bowl and whisk until light and airy. Add the remaining clarified butter in a slow drizzle while vigorously whisking the sauce, until the sauce thickens, 3 to 4 minutes. Take the bowl off the pan as soon as all the ingredients are fully incorporated. Season with a few drops of lemon juice, salt, and pepper.

Top the asparagus with the marsh samphire and salmon and pour the sauce over. Finish with freshly ground pepper.

CALORIES 850 —— FAT 84 G —— SAT FAT 44 G —— CARBS 5 G
SUGARS 3 G —— PROTEIN 24 G —— SODIUM 912 MG —— FIBER 2 G

TURNIP GREEN MASH
with Bacalhau

Mashed potatoes are the perfect Dutch comfort food. We have amazing potato varieties in our little country, which we love to mash with all kinds of vegetables. The most famous version is made with kale, endive, and carrot. Here, I share my favorite recipe with turnip greens and bacalhau, for a Portuguese twist. Bacalhau is dried and salted cod that's hugely popular in Portugal. It shouldn't be confused with stockfish, which is the unsalted dried version. To desalt and rehydrate the bacalhau, you need to soak the fish in water for about 24 hours.

SERVES 2
SOAKING TIME: 24 HOURS
PREPARATION TIME: 30 MINUTES

6 ounces (180 g) bacalhau (dried, salted cod)
17 to 18 ounces (500 g) starchy potatoes, peeled
Salt and pepper, to taste
3 tablespoons milk
2½ tablespoons butter
10 ounces (300 g) turnip greens
½ teaspoon grated nutmeg
1 tablespoon capers, rinsed and drained

Soak the bacalhau in a large bowl with plenty of cold water for 24 hours. Refresh the water every 6 hours.

Fill a large pot with water and add the potatoes and 1 teaspoon salt. Bring to a boil and cook until tender, 15 to 20 minutes.

Meanwhile, drain the fish. Fill a small saucepan with cold water, add the fish, and bring to a boil over medium-high heat. Lower the heat and simmer until the fish begins to fall apart, 10 minutes. Drain the bacalhau, remove the bones, and break the fish into pieces. Set aside.

Warm the milk in a small saucepan.

Drain the potatoes and return them to the pan to steam dry. Mash the potatoes with a potato ricer or masher. Add the warm milk and butter. Add the bacalhau, turnip greens, and nutmeg, and stir to combine. Sprinkle with freshly ground pepper and scatter the capers on top. Season with more salt if you like, but be careful as the bacalhau is very salty.

CALORIES 307 —— FAT 17 G. —— SAT FAT 10 G —— CARBS 19 G
SUGARS 4 G —— PROTEIN 24 G —— SODIUM 1,835 MG —— FIBER 9 G

CHINESE-STYLE VEGETABLES
with Prawns in Hoisin Sauce

I'm a big fan of Chinese food, which gave me the inspiration for this dish with hoisin, which means "seafood" in Cantonese.

SERVES 2
PREPARATION TIME: 20 MINUTES

7 ounces (200 g) Chinese dried wheat or rice noodles

1 tablespoon plus 1 teaspoon raw sesame oil

2 garlic cloves, sliced

¾-inch (2 cm) piece of ginger, peeled and sliced

1 red chile, seeded and finely chopped, plus extra for garnish

8 to 10 tiger prawns, heads removed, peeled, and deveined

7 ounces (200 g) Chinese broccoli

7 ounces (200 g) baby bok choy

2 scallions, cut into 1-inch (2.5 cm) pieces

1 tablespoon fish sauce

2 tablespoons hoisin sauce

1 tablespoon rice vinegar

1 tablespoon soy sauce

Chinese five-spice powder

Cook the noodles according to package directions, drain, and rinse in water. Mix in 1 teaspoon of the sesame oil, so they don't stick together. Set aside.

Place a wok over high heat and add the remaining 1 tablespoon sesame oil. Sauté the garlic, ginger, and chile for 30 seconds, constantly moving the pan so they don't burn. Add the prawns. Stir-fry for 30 seconds before adding the broccoli, bok choy, and scallion. Cook for 1 minute. Deglaze with the fish sauce. Mix in the hoisin sauce, rice vinegar, and soy sauce. Stir in the noodles and serve immediately with a pinch of five-spice powder and the extra red chile.

CALORIES 556 —— FAT 11 G —— SAT FAT 2 G —— CARBS 96 G
SUGARS 5 G —— PROTEIN 19 G —— SODIUM 1,464 MG —— FIBER 3 G

VEGETABLES À LA GRECQUE
with Tinned Sardines

I used to work at Pierre au Palais Royal, a small Michelin-starred restaurant in Paris. It was there that I really got to know my way around classic French cuisine. Every day I would prepare a dish "à la grecque," a French cooking method in which vegetables are cooked in white wine and vegetable stock. Here, I use vegetables, saffron, and tomatoes to make the flavorful broth. Often served as a starter or appetizer, this recipe also makes a great lunch, served warm or cold on a hot summer day.

SERVES 2
PREPARATION TIME: 1 HOUR

2 small artichokes
Extra virgin olive oil
1 teaspoon coriander seeds
12 cremini mushrooms, halved or quartered
6 scallions, white parts only
1 celery stalk, thinly sliced
½ zucchini, cut into strips (I used yellow zucchini)
2 garlic cloves, sliced
1 teaspoon tomato paste
Generous ¾ cup (200 ml) white wine
Juice of 1 lemon
½ teaspoon ground saffron
6 flat-leaf parsley sprigs
2 thyme sprigs
1 rosemary sprig
2 bay leaves
One 4.2-ounce (120 g) can of sardines in olive oil, drained
2 basil sprigs, leaves only

Carefully cut the stems off the artichokes. Cut away the leaves at the top with a sharp knife until you reach the heart. Pare away the leaves at the bottom. Slice off the top of the artichoke until you get to the choke. Scoop out the fibrous interior until only the heart remains. Cut it into quarters. Repeat with the remaining artichoke.

Heat 2 tablespoons of olive oil in a large saucepan over medium-high heat. Add the coriander seeds, followed by the mushrooms, scallions, celery, zucchini, and garlic. Stir-fry for 1 minute before adding the tomato paste. Stir-fry for 1 minute more, then deglaze with the wine.

Add the lemon juice and saffron. Stir until everything is well combined before adding the artichoke hearts. Add a generous ¾ cup (200 ml) of water, or enough to just cover the vegetables. Make a bouquet garni by tying the parsley, thyme, rosemary, and bay leaves together with a piece of kitchen twine and add it to the pan. Simmer over low heat until the vegetables are tender, about 10 minutes. Turn off the heat and remove the bouquet garni. Add the sardines to the pan and let them warm briefly.

Serve the dish from the pan, garnished with the basil leaves, or divide the vegetables, fish, and juice between two plates and garnish.

CALORIES 345 —— FAT 20 G —— SAT FAT 3 G —— CARBS 13 G
SUGARS 5 G —— PROTEIN 16 G —— SODIUM 370 MG —— FIBER 3 G

THE
BASICS

There are plenty of good ready-to-use stocks, curry pastes, and sauces available these days. But isn't it more fun to make your own? Trust me, they do taste better. Prepare them in bulk and you can use some and freeze the rest.

STOCKS

I use vegetable and/or fish stock in several recipes in this book. It's good to always have some on hand in your freezer, especially in ice cube trays, so you can measure out just the right amount. These keep for up to 3 months in the freezer and 2 to 3 days in the fridge. If you have no time to make your own, you can of course use ready-made stock or bouillon cubes. In that case, do bear in mind that the salt may be a bit overpowering. The recipes here don't call for any salt, as I prefer to do the seasoning in the dishes themselves.

VEGETABLE STOCK

MAKES 3 QUARTS (3 L)

3 yellow onions, coarsely chopped
2 leeks, roots trimmed, coarsely chopped
2 carrots, peeled and coarsely chopped
2 celery stalks, coarsely chopped
1 celeriac (celery root), peeled and cut into chunks
3 bay leaves
1 bunch of flat-leaf parsley
10 black peppercorns

Place the onions, leeks, carrots, celery, and celeriac in a large pot and pour in 6 quarts (6 L) of water. Add the bay leaves, parsley, and peppercorns.

Bring everything to a boil over medium-high heat. Simmer until the liquid has reduced by half, 2 to 3 hours. Strain the stock through a sieve lined with a clean kitchen towel or cheesecloth.

FISH STOCK

MAKES 3 QUARTS (3 L)

1 tablespoon butter
2 yellow onions, coarsely chopped
1 leek, roots trimmed, coarsely chopped
1 carrot, peeled and coarsely chopped
1 celery stalk, coarsely chopped
5½ pounds (2.5 kg) white fish bones and heads, gills removed, rinsed and chopped
¼ cup (60 ml) white wine
1 bunch of flat-leaf parsley
2 bay leaves
6 black peppercorns

Place a large pot over medium-high heat and melt the butter. Fry the onion, leek, carrot, and celery for 3 to 4 minutes, until translucent. Add the fish bones and stir-fry for 2 minutes before adding the 3 quarts (3 L) of water, the wine, parsley, bay leaves, and peppercorns. Make sure the pieces of fish are all covered. Bring to a boil.

Lower the heat as soon as the water starts bubbling, so it remains just below the boiling point. Skim the foam that rises to the surface.

After 25 minutes, strain the stock through a sieve lined with a clean kitchen towel or cheesecloth. Make sure the stock is completely cold before freezing.

SHELLFISH STOCK

MAKES 3 QUARTS (3 L)

2 tablespoons light olive oil
About 9 pounds (4 kg) shellfish shells and heads
3 yellow onions, coarsely chopped
1 leek, roots trimmed, coarsely chopped
1 carrot, peeled and coarsely chopped
1 celery stalk, coarsely chopped
1 fennel bulb, coarsely chopped
2 tablespoons tomato paste
Scant ¼ cup (50 ml) brandy
Scant ½ cup (100 ml) white wine
1 bunch of flat-leaf parsley
2 bay leaves
6 black peppercorns

Heat the oil in a large pot over high heat. Stir-fry the shellfish shells and heads for 4 to 5 minutes, until fragrant. Add the onions, leek, carrot, celery, and fennel and cook until slightly softened, 2 minutes. Add the tomato paste and stir 1 minute to remove acidity, before deglazing with the brandy. Add the white wine, pour in 3 quarts (3 L) of water, and bring to a boil. Add the parsley, bay leaves, and peppercorns. Bring to a boil.

Lower the heat as soon as the water starts bubbling, so it remains just below the boiling point. Skim off any foam that rises to the surface.

After 30 minutes, strain the stock through a sieve lined with a clean kitchen towel or cheesecloth. Make sure the stock is completely cold before freezing.

COURT BOUILLON

Court bouillon is often used for poaching shellfish.

MAKES 3 QUARTS (3 L)

2 yellow onions, coarsely chopped
1 carrot, peeled and coarsely chopped
2 leeks, roots trimmed, coarsely chopped
1 celery stalk, coarsely chopped
1 cup (240 ml) white wine
2 tablespoons white wine vinegar
½ bunch of flat-leaf parsley
2 bay leaves
8 black peppercorns

Place the onions, carrot, leeks, celery, wine, vinegar, parsley, bay leaves, and peppercorns in a large pot. Add 3 quarts (3 L) of water and bring to a boil. Lower the heat as soon as the water starts bubbling, so it remains just below the boiling point. Simmer gently for 20 to 25 minutes. Strain through a sieve. Make sure the bouillon is completely cold before freezing.

CURRY PASTES

I love making curries. They're not only delicious, but also incredibly quick to prepare. I like to have a few curry pastes on hand. You can certainly find good ready-to-use curry pastes in stores, but it's more fun to make your own. As far as ingredients go, there are no hard-and-fast rules—treat these recipes as a stepping-stone for putting together your own "perfect" curry. Include the chile seeds if you like it very hot; remove them for a milder version. All three pastes are made in the same way.

RED CURRY PASTE

MAKES ABOUT ½ CUP (150 G)

1 yellow onion, coarsely chopped
1 lemongrass stalk, white part only, coarsely chopped
4 garlic cloves, coarsely chopped
¾-inch (2 cm) piece of ginger, peeled and coarsely chopped
4 red chiles, stems removed
3 makrut lime leaves
½ bunch of cilantro
½ teaspoon ground turmeric
1 teaspoon tomato paste
Zest of 1 lime
¼ cup (60 ml) sunflower oil
Salt, to taste

YELLOW CURRY PASTE

MAKES ABOUT ½ CUP (150 G)

1 yellow onion, coarsely chopped
1 lemongrass stalk, white part only, coarsely chopped
4 garlic cloves, coarsely chopped
¾-inch (2 cm) piece of ginger, peeled and coarsely chopped
4 yellow chiles, stems removed
1 yellow bell pepper, seeded and coarsely chopped
3 makrut lime leaves
1 teaspoon ground turmeric
Zest of 1 lime
¼ cup (60 ml) sunflower oil
Salt, to taste

GREEN CURRY PASTE

MAKES ABOUT ½ CUP (150 G)

1 yellow onion, coarsely chopped
2 scallions, coarsely chopped
1 lemongrass stalk, white part only, coarsely chopped
4 garlic cloves, coarsely chopped
¾-inch (2 cm) piece of ginger, peeled and coarsely chopped
4 green chiles, stems removed
3 makrut lime leaves
1 bunch of cilantro
Zest of 1 lime
Scant ¼ cup (50 ml) sunflower oil
Salt, to taste

Blend the ingredients together in a food processor, blender, or mortar to form a paste; you can make it as smooth or as coarse as you wish. Season with salt.

MAYONNAISE-BASED SAUCES

Fish is traditionally served with mayonnaise-based sauces. You may have noticed that I often opt for lighter sauces made with yogurt, but that doesn't change the fact that a good homemade mayonnaise is always delicious. I like mine to be on the tart side, but feel free to experiment with the amounts of vinegar and lemon juice.

MAYONNAISE

MAKES ABOUT 1 CUP (240 ML)

1 egg yolk
2 teaspoons Dijon mustard
1 tablespoon white wine vinegar
Salt and pepper, to taste
⅔ to ¾ cup (150 to 200 ml) sunflower oil
Fresh lemon juice, to taste
Worcestershire sauce, to taste

Make sure all your ingredients are at room temperature. In a small bowl, whisk the egg yolk together with the mustard, vinegar, and a pinch of salt. Slowly add the oil, whisking constantly. The sauce is thick enough when it sticks to the whisk. Season the mayonnaise with lemon juice, Worcestershire sauce, salt, and pepper.

MARIE ROSE SAUCE

MAKES ABOUT ⅔ CUP (150 ML)

Scant ½ cup (100 ml) mayonnaise
2 tablespoons heavy cream, whipped until thickened
2 tablespoons ketchup
1 tablespoon whiskey
Pinch of cayenne pepper
Salt and pepper, to taste (optional)

Combine the ingredients in a small bowl. Season with salt and pepper, if desired.

RÉMOULADE

MAKES A SCANT ½ CUP (100 ML)

¼ cup (60 ml) Mayonnaise (see this page)
1 shallot, finely diced
1 tablespoon capers, rinsed and drained, finely chopped
1 gherkin, finely chopped
3 chives, finely chopped
2 flat-leaf parsley sprigs, leaves only, finely chopped
Salt and pepper, to taste (optional)

Combine the ingredients in a small bowl. Season with salt and pepper, if desired.

TARTAR SAUCE

Tartar sauce has the same ingredients as rémoulade sauce, with the addition of a very finely chopped hard-cooked egg.

MAKES A SCANT ½ CUP (100 ML)

¼ cup (60 ml) mayonnaise
1 shallot, finely diced
1 tablespoon capers, rinsed and drained, finely chopped
1 gherkin, finely chopped
3 chives, finely chopped
2 flat-leaf parsley sprigs, leaves only, finely chopped
1 egg, boiled for about 8 minutes, cooled, peeled, and minced
Salt and pepper, to taste

Combine the ingredients in a small bowl.

AÏOLI

MAKES ABOUT ¾ CUP (180 ML)

2 garlic cloves, coarsely chopped
½ slice of white bread, crust removed, cut into small pieces
Salt and pepper, to taste
1 egg yolk
½ cup (125 ml) light olive oil
Fresh lemon juice, to taste

Mash the garlic and bread with a pinch of salt in a mortar to form a paste. Whisk in the egg yolk. Slowly add the olive oil, stirring constantly. The aïoli is ready when it has a texture similar to mayonnaise. Season with lemon juice, salt, and pepper.

ROUILLE

MAKES ABOUT ¾ CUP (180 ML)

½ slice of white bread, crust removed, cut into small pieces
1 garlic clove, coarsely chopped
5 saffron threads
½ teaspoon cayenne pepper
1 egg yolk
½ cup (125 ml) light olive oil
Fresh lemon juice, to taste
Salt, to taste

Mash the bread with the garlic and saffron in a mortar to form a smooth paste. Add the cayenne pepper and whisk in the egg yolk. Slowly add the olive oil, stirring constantly. Keep whisking until the texture is similar to that of mayonnaise. Season with lemon juice and salt.

PRESERVED LEMONS & LIMES

Preserved lemon or lime can really enhance a dish. It's widely used in Middle Eastern cooking, but it can also be a tasty addition to recipes from other parts of the world.

MAKES 8 PRESERVED LEMONS OR LIMES

⅓ cup (70 g) coarse sea salt
8 lemons or limes

Spoon 2 tablespoons of the salt into a sterilized quart-size (945 ml) mason jar. Cut an X into each lemon or lime, a bit like cutting four wedges, but don't cut all the way through—stop about two-thirds down. Generously fill the incisions with salt. Add the fruits to the jar, packing them as tightly together as possible.

Add the rest of the salt and fill the jar with water; make sure the lemons are submerged. Seal the jar tightly. Store the jar in a cold and dark place for 3 to 4 weeks. The fruits are ready when softened.

TIPS & TRICKS
HOW TO OPEN AN OYSTER

While it may seem difficult to shuck an oyster, it's actually not that hard. You can buy special gloves for protection, but with the following instructions you should be able to open your oysters easily and safely.

1 Place a kitchen towel on your work surface and place an oyster on it, flat side up.

2 Fold the other half of the towel over the oyster, leaving only the narrow end of the shell sticking out.

3 Insert the tip of the oyster knife into the hinge between the two shells.

4 Work the tip of the knife up and down and back and forth until the oyster opens.

5 Cup the oyster in your hand, keeping the rounded side down. Lift the top shell slightly and slowly run the knife along the inside while scraping the top of the shell to release the muscle. Discard the top shell.

6 Release the oyster meat from the bottom shell by cutting through the muscle. Try not to spill any of the oyster liquor. Remove any bits of shell, if necessary. Serve on a bed of ice or coarse sea salt.

HOW TO SHELL A
LARGE PRAWN OR SHRIMP

I recommend you only buy prawns and shrimp in the shell, as they retain the most flavor. Some recipes call for shelled prawns, so here's a step-by-step guide on how best to shell them.

1 Hold the prawn's head and slowly twist it off its body.

2 Insert your thumbs underneath the shell and loosen it.

3 Peel off the shell in segments until you get to the tail.

4 When you reach the tail, pinch and pull so it comes off. The prawn is now shelled.

5 Make a superficial incision along the back of the prawn.

6 Remove the intestinal tract or vein with the tip of your knife.

HOW TO CLEAN A SMALL ROUND FISH

Small round fish include the likes of sardines and anchovies. Use a small kitchen knife for these delicate fish.

1 Hold the fish's head in one hand and a small kitchen knife in the other.

2 Scrape the scales off the fish with the blunt side of the blade, working from the tail up to the head.

3 Discard the scales.

4 Place one hand on top of the fish and, with the other, slice open its belly. Cut up to the head.

5 Remove the guts by scraping them out of the cavity with your knife.

6 Thoroughly rinse the cavity and skin under cold running water.

HOW TO FILLET A SMALL ROUND FISH

Once the fish has been cleaned, you can fillet it using a fillet knife or a medium chef's knife. I use the following technique.

1 Place the fish on a cutting board and make a vertical incision right behind the ear, down to the bone.

2 Place your other hand on top of the fish and turn your knife from vertical to horizontal.

3 Cut away the fillet in one clean sweep, starting at the head, all the way to the tail. Slide your knife as close as possible along the spine.

4 Flip the fish and repeat step 3.

5 Tidy the fillets up along the edges.

6 The fillets are ready to be used.

HOW TO CLEAN A LARGE ROUND FISH

Your fishmonger can take care of this for you, if you prefer, but do ask for the head and bones so you can make your own fish stock. You'll need kitchen scissors and a scaling knife to clean larger fish.

1 Cut off the pectoral fins with a pair of kitchen scissors.

2 Trim away the pelvic and dorsal fins.

3 Hold the fish by the tail and, with your other hand, scrape off the scales, working from the tail toward the head.

4 Slide the knife into the anus (the small vent about one-third of the way in from the tail) and slice open the belly, not too deep, up to the head.

5 Use your hand—and your knife, if necessary—to scrape the guts out of the cavity.

6 Rinse the cavity under cold running water.

HOW TO FILLET A LARGE ROUND FISH

I use the following technique to fillet a large round fish. Make sure to use a very sharp knife.

1 Make an incision on both sides of the fish, cutting from the belly side to the top of the head, down to the spine.

2 Firmly hold the fish by inserting your hand into the belly cavity. Starting from the head and moving the knife along the spine, make a ¼-inch-deep (6 mm) incision.

3 Repeat, slicing a little deeper from head to tail until you hit the middle bone.

4 At about a third of the way in from the tail (at the level of the fish's anus), insert the knife horizontally through the fish and cut the fillet away from the spine, working toward the tail.

5 Starting from the head, cut the fillet until it comes away from the ribs. Repeat steps 2, 3, and 4 on the other side of the fish.

6 Remove any pin bones with tweezers, if necessary, and tidy the fillets up along the edges.

HOW TO SKIN
A FISH FILLET

Many recipes call for skin-on fish fillets, but for some dishes it's better to use fillets without skin. Use a knife at least as long as the width of the fillet.

1 Place the fillet on a cutting board, skin side down. Make an incision with your knife on one side.

2 Dab your fingers in some water and then salt to get a better grip on the skin.

3 Firmly hold the incision. Place the knife diagonally on the skin and cut the first part of the fillet away from the skin.

4 Turn the knife so it's horizontal. Slowly slide it, moving backward and forward, along the skin.

5 Cut the entire fillet away from the skin.

6 The fillet is ready to be used.

HOW TO CLEAN
A SQUID

Many squid recipes call for the tube (the body) and the tentacles. The following steps show you the easiest way to clean a squid or cuttlefish.

1 Cut the tentacles off the head, just above the eyes.

2 Remove the small hard piece of cartilage (the mouth) from the center of the tentacles and discard it.

3 Hold the squid in one hand, and with the other pull the entrails from the body, including the ink sac.

4 Remove the long, hard spine from the fish by tugging at it (it's the bit that looks like plastic).

5 Remove the skin by pulling it off, starting from the wider end and working your way down. A slightly blunt knife can help with this.

6 Rinse the squid under cold running water.

ACKNOWLEDGMENTS

Thank you!

This is a book I'm immensely proud of. I feel privileged to have worked with my dream team again. The COVID-19 pandemic made it far from easy, especially in terms of logistics, so I'm all the more grateful and pleased that we made it happen together with so much passion and fun.

David Loftus, my buddy, many, many thanks for your beautiful photographs. You're able to visualize the dishes I make, and what I feel and want to communicate, like no other. Love you!

Inge Tichelaar, our friendship goes back a long time. You're not only this book's food stylist, but above all, my critical conscience and mental coach. Sometimes we lock horns, but always with the aim of jointly achieving the best possible end result. Thank you so much. Love you!

Thank you, Daan de Rooij, for your meticulous work in the kitchen and for your inspiration. With you by my side, it's always a blast! Many thanks to Alyssa Vukaj for your assistance on cooking days. Thank you, Tonin Vukaj, for your Italian inspiration and help.

Tijs Koelemeijer: I'm thrilled with the way this book has turned out. Thank you for the amazing design and illustrations, but even more so for being my sparring partner. It's great that we've made another book together.

Mitchell van Voorbergen, thank you so much for your share in the book's photography and your flexibility and ability to adapt. Working with you again was terrific.

Everybody at Fontaine Uitgevers: thank you! My special thanks to Francis Wehkamp for her confidence in this project. Many thanks to Kelly Heeren for your editorial work. Thank you, Laurie Branderhorst, for the promotional activities around this book. And a big shout-out to Harold Zwaal for the enthusiasm with which you got everybody involved.

Lars Hamer: thank you for the culinary edits. You're a star! Thank you to Angela Severs and Christel Vondermans for your work on the nutritional values.

Josh Niland, thank you so much for your kind words.

Many thanks to Olivia Peluso, who edited this book in English in such a great way. You have really challenged me, and I like that a lot! Thank you, Laura Vroomen, for the translation and critical support, and many thanks to Matthew Lore of The Experiment in New York for having the trust and belief in me to publish another one of my books in the US. Thank you, Jennifer Hergenroeder, for the PR work, and Beth Bugler for the wonderful cover design. Thank you, Suzanne Fass, for copy editing. So happy with you all at The Experiment! Thank you!

Thank you to everybody at Sea Tales, especially my business partner and friend Harm Jan van Dijk and our lovely local US representative Kim Yorio. Special thanks again to Kim and Aimee Bianca of YC Media in New York for your amazing PR support. Thank you to the amazing folks at Ambactus Group who have made this fantastic Sea Tales dream happen in America.

A big thanks to the fantastic professionals at Viscenter Volendam: Jack and Jordy Schilder, thank you so much. Marcus Polman, thank you for your PR work and your mental support. Thank you to

Maurice Kroon at House of Talent for overseeing this project.

And for letting me use their beautiful styling props, I'd like to thank: my dear mom and stepfather, Annelie and René Thuring; Kookwinkel Duikelman Amsterdam; my mate Xander Bueno de Mesquita; and Henk Tomson at "Maak-Henk." Berend te Voortwis and everybody at Lindenhoff: thank you for your hospitality.

Dear Bernadien: I hope we get to eat lots more veggies & fish together. Love you.

And above all I'd like to thank my wonderful children, Bo, Juul, and Ties: for your enjoyable company while making this book, and your inspiration, love, and patience. I'm so proud of you! Love you, love you, love you!

INDEX

ABOUT THE AUTHOR

BART VAN OLPHEN is arguably the world's most passionate sustainable-fishing advocate and overall lover of fish. In 2018, his book *Bart's Fish Tales: A Fishing Adventure in Over 100 Recipes* was awarded the Gourmand World Cookbook Award for Best Seafood Cookbook and was named the Travel Cookery Book of the Year by the Edward Stanford Travel Writing Awards. He is the author of the internationally bestselling *The Tinned Fish Cookbook* and the cofounder of the fish brand Sea Tales (in the US) and Fish Tales (in Europe). You can check out his travels around the world and enjoy his cooking show on Instagram (@bartsfishtales) and YouTube (@bartsfishtales)—and at bartvanolphen.com and sea-tales.com.